The Origin and Antiquity

OF

PHYSICAL MAN

SCIENTIFICALLY CONSIDERED.

PROVING MAN TO HAVE BEEN CONTEMPORARY WITH THE MASTODON; DETAILING THE HISTORY OF HIS DEVELOPMENT FROM THE DOMAIN OF THE BRUTE, AND DISPERSION BY GREAT WAVES OF EMIGRATION FROM CENTRAL ASIA.

BY

HUDSON TUTTLE,

AUTHOR OF ARCANA OF NATURE, ETC.

BOSTON:
WILLIAM WHITE & COMPANY,
158 WASHINGTON STREET.
1866.

Stereotyped by C. J. Peters & Son,
No. 13, Washington Street.

PREFACE.

THERE are two classes of writers who produce two very distinct classes of books. The first are trained to write, as the gladiators were trained to fight, and are the present champions of the prize-ring. Libráries and encyclopædias are their weapons. The skilful use of these is their strength. They learn to polish periods, and write over other men's ideas, and by burnishing and varnishing, and a slight veneer of wording, present them so different that their authors do not recognize their own children. They do not write because they have any thing to say, but because there is honor and profit in the pen.

The second class write because they have something to say. Libraries are of little benefit to them, and because of their originality, they are not encouraged by profit. I claim no skill in modelling sentences, or in the desirable art of presenting my subjects in their most pleasing forms; nor can I claim to belong to that class who have something worthy of record to say when they write. What, then, is my apology for obtruding a book on an old and vexed theme? It is briefly this:—

I began an investigation of the philosophy of history, going downward into the strata of earlier and pre-historic races. I at length came to the question of man's origin. It struck me that on its elucidation rested the *science* of history,—at least, here was its first great problem.

The reasoning I pursued in arriving at a solution I have recorded, faithfully marking the places where research is needed, where discoveries may be expected, and where facts are wanting to fully establish the views suggested. I have sought to find the truth, and present it as clearly as possible, not to vindicate any favorite theory. In this research I have drawn largely on the works of the great scientists of the day. To Sir Charles Lyell, Darwin, Huxley, Carpentier, Pritchard, Müller, Guyot, and Agassiz, I am particularly indebted, and take pleasure in the acknowledgment.

H. T.

BOSTON, MASS., 1866.

CONTENTS.

INTRODUCTION.

Vulgar Aim of History. — How Man solves the Question of his Individual Origin and that of the Race. — The Cosmogony of Genesis imperfect. — Agassiz' Theory no better. — The Theory of Unity, if Genesis be received, untenable. — Origin of Species. — The Geological Record. — The Position of Man, and his Relations. — The Grand Ideal of Nature is Life. — What is Life? — Classifications of the Races of Men. — Of Buffon, Kant, Hunter, Netzau, Virey, Blumenbach, Desmoulins, Morton, Pickering, Bury de St. Vincent, Burke, Jacquinnot. — The Object of the Work 13

CHAPTER I.

ANTIQUITY OF MAN.

Traditionary Chronology. — Effects of Prejudice. — Fossil Man. — Imperfection of the Geological Record. — The Plan of Nature is to destroy the Products of Life. — Fossil Human Remains in the New World. — New-Orleans Skeleton, its Age calculated at 27,600 years. — Natchez Skeleton. — Human Fossils in Brazil. — Mounds of the Ohio. — In the Old World. — In the Loess of the Rhine. — In the Maastricht and Hocht Canal. — Arrow-heads of the Valley of the Somme and Seine, of England. — Caverns. — Determination of Age of Bones by Amount of Organic Matter they contain. — Cave of Durfurt. — Caves in France. — Caves of Sailenreuth, Coppingen, Kustritz; of Gower, of North Sicily. — Lake Dwellings. — Danish Seat. — Danish Shell Mounds. — Södertelzo Fossils, calculated Age 16,000 years. — Calculated Age of Arrow-heads in Peat of the Valley of the Somme 120,000 years. — Antiquity of Egyptian Civilization. — Fossil Remains of the Dog. — The Grotto of Sartel. — Summary . . 38

CHAPTER II.

RELATIONS OF MAN TO THE ANTHROPOID APES.

The Climate of the Tertiary Warm. — Whence came the Savage of the Flint Arrow-head? — Primates, no Break or Chasm between them and Man. — Fossil Primates, Dryopithecus, of the Swiss Jura, Eocene. — Linnæan Classification of PRIMATES. — Embryonic Form of the PRIMATES. — ANTHROPOID, or MAN-LIKE APES. — First Account of the PONGO.— Anatomical Structure. — The GIBBONS. — ORANG-OUTANG. — CHIMPANZEE. — GORILLA. — The Point of Man's Contact with the Animal World, the Quadrumania. — Comparison of Structure of the Hand, Foot, Vertebral Column, Pelvis, Skull, and Teeth. — Brain, Convolutions of. — Correspondence of *Fossil Human Remains*, the Engis Skull, the Neanderthall Skull. — CONCLUSIONS 66

CHAPTER III.

ORIGIN OF LANGUAGE.

The Myth of the Tower of Babel. — Is Man the only Being possessing Language? — Growth of Language illustrated in the Romance Tongues. — The Language of Animals. — Intonations of Savage Man. — Ideas of Savages. — Language the Expression of Ideas. — Polysynthesism, its Outgrowths. — Comparison with the Growth of Living Beings. — Fossil Languages a sure Guide in History. — Inevitable Growth of Language. — The Sanskrit. — Rig-Veda. — Difficulty of crossing Languages. — Rapid Changes in the Dialects of Savages. — The great Achievement of Comparative Philology, — the Discovery of an Ancient Tongue to which Sanskrit, Greek, Latin, &c., are mutually related. — Its Method of Research. — What is a just Estimate of the Affinities of Dialects? — Agassiz' Theory of Language opposed. — Conclusions. 89

CHAPTER IV.

ORGANIC AND CLIMATIC CHANGES.

Geographical Dispersion of Organic Beings in Relation to Man. — The Great Zoölogical Provinces first distinctly marked immediately antecedent to the Introduction of Man. — Cause of. — Climate of the Earth during the Tertiary. — Disappearance of Climatic Distinctions in the Secondary Strata. — ZOÖLOGICAL PROVINCES of the Earth, — the Arctic Realm, the Asiatic, the European, the African, the Australian, the Indian, the Polynesian. — Realms, how defined, how produced. — The Principles applicable to the Dispersion of Animals also applicable to the Dispersion of the Races of Men 112

CHAPTER V.

THE UNITY OF MANKIND.

Definition of *Species*. — Points of Agreement of all the Races of Men. — Longevity. — Contagious Diseases. — Color of Skin. — Color of Eyes and Hair. — Texture of Hair. — Similar Variations observed in Animals. — Albinos. — Anatomical Comparison of the Races. — Measurements and Comparison of Skulls of. — Hybridity. — Egyptian Records. — CONCLUSIONS 124

CHAPTER VI.

RELATION OF CONTINENTAL FORMS TO MAN.

Bacon's Observation. — Analogies between the Continents. — Typical Continental Form. — The Three Double Worlds. — Benefits conferred on Man by Contour of the Land. — Influence of Mountain Chains, and of Large Bodies of Water. — What is Acclimation? — Application of foregoing Principles 139

CHAPTER VII.

THE FIRST WAVES OF DISPERSION: THE ORIENTAL NEGRO, AFRICAN AND SEMITE.

The ORIENTAL NEGRO, or the Australian Race. — When originated the three Great Branches, SEMITIC, TURANIAN, ARYAN? — The SEMITIC. — Structure of Language; divided into Aramean, Hebrew, Arabian; Description of Character, Language and History of Each. — Nestorians. — Berbers. — Phœnicians. — Egyptians, Language of, Origin of, Shepherd Kings of. — Copts. — African Tribes of Semitic Origin: Haussa, Gallas, Berberins, Fellatah, Mandingoes, Yoloffs. — AFRICAN RACE. — Description of, Origin of. — Divided into two Great Families, KAFFER and HOTTENTOT. — Language of Africa. — The DAMARAS. — The KAFFER. — The HOTTENTOT. — Description of, Language of, and History of Each. 150

CHAPTER VIII.

THE NORTH TURANIAN RACES.

Name, Derivation of. —Which are the Autochthonic, the Aborignal Races?— Wide extent of the Turanian Family. — Characteristics of Languages, Agglutination.— Successive Waves. — The Chinese.— Iberians.— Lapps. — Finns.— Permians.— Votiaks.— Tscheremisses. — Voguls. — Ostiaks, &c. — Samoiedes. — The Mongolians. — Turkish Race. — Turkomans.— Usbeks. — Kirgis. — Yakuts. — The TUNGUSIANS. — Mandshus. — Ostiaks of the Yenisei. — Yakagers. — Kamtschadales. — Aino. — Coreans. — Japanese.— Lew-Chew Islanders.— American Indians, Similarity of.— Unity of, Origin of. — Origin of Indian Tribes. — The INCAS and AZTECS, from whence Derived. — Relations between the Indians and Northern Asiatics. — The Destiny of the Red Race. — Turanians of the Caucasus: GEORGIANS, CIRCASSIANS, ABYSSINIANS 179

CHAPTER IX.

THE SOUTH TURANIAN RACES.

The "Hill Tribes," or Dravidians of Hindostan. — Pritchard's Failure. — The BHILLS. — Pariahs. — Gonds. — Peoples of the Valleys of the Ganges and Brahmapootra. — Siamese. — Taï Tribes. — Bengalese. — Thugs. — THE POLYNESIANS, From whence Dispersed? — MALAYS. — They are the Nomads of the Sea. — Vast Geographical Extent of this Race. — Turanian Fragments in Africa. — Extent of Dispersion not an Argument against Community of Descent 200

CHAPTER X.

THE ARYAN RACES.

Who are Aryans? — Origin of, and Attainments in Civilization before the Separation of its Component Races. — A Sketch of the Method of Linguistic Research. — The *Vendidad*, and Zend-avesta. — Date of the Foundation of the Median Empire. — INDIC BRANCH. — Prakrit, Sanskrit, and Zend. — The Gypsies. — THE IRANIC, or PERSIAN, BRANCH. — Effect of the religious system of ZOROASTER. — The Language of the MAGI. — Pure Persian. — The Afghans. — Buchars. — Kurds. — Belooches. — Armenians. — Assetes. — Parsees. — Guebres. — NORTHERN BRANCH. — Pelasgi. — Thracians. — Kelts. — Sclavonians. — Lithuranians. — THE TEUTONIC RACES. — Their History, Customs, and Languages. — From whence came the Waves of People that devastated Rome? — Goths. — Franks. — Saxons. — Alemanii. — Vandals, Longobards. — Huns. — Relations of Languages. — CONCLUSIONS 209

CHAPTER XI.

NATURAL SELECTION IN THE ANIMAL WORLD.

The Exalted Position of Man. — The Arguments for the Origin of Species of Animals, by Natural Causes, apply to the Origin of Races of Men. — Consequences of the Introduction of one Being, and its Increase. — The Antagonist of Multiplication. — The Struggle for Life. — No Catastrophe, but Certain and Perpetual Change. — Illustrations. — The same Laws applicable to Past as to Present Beings. — The two Antagonistic Forces. — Selection by Man. — Wherein different from that of Nature. — Selection by Nature. — Application to Man 235

CHAPTER XII.

CONCLUSION.

The Geographical Seat of Man's Origin. — Natural Selection applied to Man 250

THE
ORIGIN AND ANTIQUITY OF MAN,
SCIENTIFICALLY CONSIDERED.

INTRODUCTION.

Vulgar Aim of History. — How Man solves the Question of his Individual Origin and that of the Race. — The Cosmogony of Genesis imperfect. — Agassiz' Theory no better. — The Theory of Unity, if Genesis be received, untenable. — Origin of Species. — The Geological Record. — The Position of Man, and his Relations. — The Grand Ideal of Nature is Life. — What is Life? — Classifications of the Races of Men. — Of Buffon, Kant, Hunter, Netzau, Virey, Blumenbach, Desmoulins, Morton, Pickering, Bury de St. Vincent, Burke, Jacquinnot. — The Object of the Work.

History has been content to chronicle the actions of mankind, and not until yesterday has it sought to philosophize on the events it recorded. Philosophy is avoided by the low aim of the simple narrations called histories. To reduce all the facts of the past to wide generalizations, so as to take in at a grasp the entire sum of human activity, is the work of to-day. The origin of man lies at the foundation of the philosophy of history, yet history affords little aid in the solution of this most complex problem. Before it opens its annals, the scaffolding has been torn away from the comparatively completed world; and little trace remains to tell us how the structure was reared. Individual existence is too brief, and the historic period too limited, to allow us to pierce the mists which conceal the origin of passing events. We are inexplicable enigmas. We stand up complete, and even tradition speaks in fable of our beginning.

We learn of our individual origin by observing the origin of individuals like ourselves; and, by analogous observations of the wider branches, — the savage types thrown off in his growth, — we can learn the pathway of man's ascent.

Hitherto tradition has held the position of positive knowledge. Revelation, too, has been distorted to the unholy office of fettering science. The question under discussion is not a theological one, unless the theologian pleases to make it so; and, should he so please, the task to him is willingly accorded. Here it is inadmissible, for we deal with facts; and, as necessarily the conclusions of truthful reasoning stand side by side with truthful revelation, we shall take no pains to harmonize one with the other, but pursue our course to its results. For a moment only will I dwell on the salient points of the connection between the account of the creation contained in Genesis, and that of science.

View it in whatever light we please, it is a strange fact that all the superior races of men have a more or less defined feeling of universal brotherhood. The common fatherhood is deeply felt, and unquestioningly received. Its rejection appears to be the result of false theories, or a mistaken notion of the manner in which this brotherhood resulted. Much bitterness has been manifested on both sides of this question without a step of advancement.

The literal interpretation of the account contained in Genesis is now held by the best authorities as untenable. It is allegorical; and, as each authority explains the allegory as his fancy dictates, or in such a manner as matches it with his theory, it has little scientific value, — at least until better understood.

The explanation of Agassiz, that mankind were first created in nations, so far from solving the question, renders it more confused. It carries us no nearer the real cause; and, if we were before unable to account for the birth of the first pair, equally unable are we now of accounting for that of the mighty races and nations which start into being over the whole globe. Every great province of the earth has its own fauna, and its own race of men. "These," says the great naturalist, "are autochthonic, and were created where they are found; and consequently there is no great tie of common origin, but each received birth by an independent creation." It is true, as he states, that the correspondence between the races of mankind and the faunas which, as it were, underlie them is very remarkable: "One which cannot fail to throw light on the origin of the differences existing among men, since it shows that man's physical nature is modified by the same laws as that of animals, and that any general results obtained from the animal kingdom regarding the organic differences of its various types must also apply to man," an inference hereafter to be applied. This conclusion is followed by the startling assumption that such diversity of origin does not conflict with the unity of the races and the common brotherhood of man. The two alternatives he presents are, birth from a common stock, and that all subsequent changes are the results of diversity of surroundings, or that these changes result from a direct exertion of miraculous power on the part of the Creator, and their distribution a part of his plan, "and human races, down to their specialization as nations, are distinct primordial forms of the type of man." Such are the conclusions to which one of the greatest scientific men of the age has arrived. After striving all his life to attain the real cause of phenomena, he quietly refers every thing he cannot solve to miraculous agency, — a conclusion unworthy of the age.

Granting man to have been created six thousand years ago, the Pritchard school have a bad cause to defend; and, admitting such to be the true chronology, the conclusions of Agassiz must be received. If it be denied, then both fall with all the host of dependent writers. Even the supporters of unity have endeavored to prove that this unity centred in a single pair within historic time, and hence have not taken a step towards the solution of the question; for, if mankind are referred to a single pair, created perfect, that pair, isolated as they necessarily must be from surrounding creation, must have been miraculously created.

Great laws underlie and permeate creation, on whose atlas shoulders all things are supported. No province of nature is exempt from their sway, and in no case are they for a moment set aside. Ignorance only sees miracle and direct exertion of power. We know that we exist by the power of fixed and immutable principles, and consequently we must have originated through their agency. We know that the universe is a unity of forces; that the realm of life is governed throughout its vast extent by fixed principles, which, applying to all beings, to the highest and the lowest, bind them all together, and infallibly point to a common source.

It has been well remarked, that, if we grant the common origin of mankind, we must also that of the animal world, and be pushed to the transcendental philosophy of Lamarck. We accept the premises, and the greater portion of the philosophy of one of the greatest naturalists Europe has produced. It is on this basis that the proofs of the common origin of the animal world have a direct bearing on the origin of mankind.

Species of animals and plants have their origin in the lowest forms of life; and their progress, and the characteristics which distinguish them, are results of physical conditions combined with the peculiarities of the beings on which they are exerted.* This is supported by a vast array of facts drawn from organic nature. The changes produced by domestication and the *artificial selection* of man; the still more potent force of *natural selection* by which only the most vigorous individuals are preserved; the study of transitional varieties; the laws of hybridity and variation, — all afford immutable pillars of support to this theory, which applies with equal truth to man.

The geological records of the earth substantiate the foregoing conclusions, and prove that progress is the plan of creation in this world. In order to under-

* See Darwin's Origin of Species.

stand the idea of progress introduced into this work, and show how man is indissolubly united to the animal realm, I pause to condense in a few sentences the progress of the earth and its living tenants as revealed by the light of the only rational theory yet promulgated.

From the increasing temperature as the earth is penetrated toward the centre, the volcanic character presented by the moon, the arrangement of the solar system, it has been theoretically advanced with almost the conclusiveness of mathematical demonstration, that the earth was once in a fluid state from ignition, and farther yet in a gaseous condition. Inherent forces outwrought a solar system from this primitive gaseous chaos. This was the first state of advancement, from which a steady progress is observed to the present. The rock-volume of earth, as read by the light of science, presents a constant succession of the grandest advances. A crust cools over the fiery globe, on the jagged surface of which, when sufficiently solid, water condenses from the atmosphere, running down into the hollows, forming boiling pools. These unite, forming shallow seas, which when sufficiently cooled, living beings are generated.

Not the highest forms of life, however, but the lowest; mere masses of cells having the appearance of irregular fragments of jelly. Billions of ages rolled away into the past eternity before a single vertebrate animal came; and when they were introduced it was only the lowest forms, — the fishes, and the lowest of the fishes.

Then came frog-like, bird-like, and marine reptiles;

the huge and terrible saurians of the old world, spanning in multitudinous shapes several vast geological ages. Then came gigantic mammals, the latest types of which were the mastodon and mammoth. With the latter came the existing fauna, with man as its highest type.

From this brief outline we can gather an idea of the position of man, and the relations he sustains to the inorganic and organic creations beneath him.

A more extensive or interesting subject for study could not well be selected. Standing as man does between the brutes of the field on one hand, and the angels of light on the other; forming a bridge spanning the gulf between material forms, which perish, and those who bask in eternal light,—an investigation of his relations reaches through all grades of intelligence; through all forms of matter; from the pebble beaten by the surf on the ocean's shore, to the throne of Deity.

For man is the representative of the universe; the grand archetype of creation, in whom all elements, principles, and forms are unitized.

The grand idea of Nature is life. The highest evolution of creative energy is a perfect living being. Strange, incomprehensible, is life and its laws. I know not if an *archangel*, ripe in the lore of a thousand ages, could answer the question what it is better than a child. We may understand many of its laws, and necessary *conditions*, but its *final* causes remain sealed; and the hand of science vainly essays to break and read its arcana.

What is life? It is the turmoil of elemental forces,

the rush of storms, the crash of ocean, the sparkle of sunlight, the whirl of suns and worlds; for what we call inorganic nature, is really organic; and suns and worlds are globules floating in the great arteries of the universal system. The principles we see manifested in the harmony of arrangement, the beautiful adaptation of means to ends, are the *thoughts* of that universal whole.

The imponderable agents of light, heat, magnetism, electricity, are the messengers and executors of those thoughts. We call these manifestations life, for they correspond to the life of a living being. It is the gigantic exhibition of identical forces concentrated and individualized, but *dwarfed* in ourselves.*

When we see the whirlwind rushing past, or view the terrible energies of the ocean, or gaze into the profound and awfully silent depths of the starry night, all our emotions are derived from the instinctive feeling of unity and brotherhood with these. The rave of the storm-swept sea beats on our hearts, and finds responsive strains; the mad violence of the tempest awakes the consciousness of slumbering tempests in our brain; and the grandeur of starry worlds produces a corresponding grandeur of being within *us*.

For our being is cosmopolitan. There is nothing but what we have been elementally; and, elementally and organically, all things are represented in us.

Living beings are the separations of these forces, so terrible and gigantic in the world of elements, their individualization. How this was *effected* would require the history of the globe: the geological hieroglyphics of the great rock-volume of earth alone can

* See Arcana of Nature.

reveal the biography of life from the point where it touches the geometrically formed crystal, and its ascension to the myriad forms we behold around us.

Does the heart pulsate? it does so by the same force by which our earth is chained to the sun, and rolled along its orbit. Does the blood circulate? so does the aqueous fluid of our planet. The currents of wind and clouds are the arteries, rivers its veinous system, and the oceans temporary receptacles. Does the stomach digest? see how matter is digested by the earth, ever eliminated in more sublimated forms. Above all, does the brain think? *so do the elements.* See how undeviatingly they run on their missions, and with what wonderful perfection they accomplish their tasks. A continent is parched by drought: see the winds take up water from the sea, and drench it until vast Amazons and Orinocos run from its deluged back. There is too much moisture; and the winds waft it away. A chaos exists, of conflicting elements: see how, under the influence of their co-eternal attributes, they evolve worlds and suns, and harmony springs from discord, or beautiful solar systems roll out of darkness into light.

Child of the Eternal, thy being pulsates with the eternal of nature because *thou* art eternal. They awake awe in thee because of the dim consciousness that all are but accidents of thy being, to melt and vanish away as thou proceedest on thy course.

Life, as a general expression, is divided into two branches, — one characteristic of animals, the other of vegetables. We may call that common to animals and vegetables, organic life; that confined to animals, animal life. While *plants* have only life, as it were only *existing*, man has *two* distinct existences, the other and higher being differentiated through the *lower* forms of *animal* being. He possesses *two* lives, *vegetative* and *animal* life. Intricately blended as these are, they are governed by distinct and wholly separate laws.

Through the organic laws man reaches down to the plant, and becomes brother with flower, fruit, and tree; acknowledges closest relationship with fucoids of the sea, palms of tropic climes, and alpine pines. As the organic functions are internal, they are purely selfish, and only act to build up the organic structure by the processes of *assimilation*, as digestion, circulation, nutrition, and, in the equally necessary processes of its *destruction*, as exhalation, secretion, and excretion. These functions are held in common by man and plants. They are independent of mind, and proceed uninterruptedly, the mind being unconscious of their operations during their normal state. His animal life is external, bringing him in contact with other objects. It is his conscious existence.

If we examine anatomically the organs by which these two lives are carried on, we shall find that while the organs of purely organic life are very *irregular*, as stomach, liver, &c., and their functions being equally well performed however great their departure from the common type, the organs of *animal* life are remarkably *symmetrical*, as the brain, organs of vision, hearing, &c., and the slightest departure is accompanied by impaired functions, or entire destruction.

These processes go on normally, wholly unheeded

by the mind. Its powers are not wasted on the most important organic functions, but are reserved for those of conscious existence.

The animal life is not necessarily unintermittent, but the reverse. Vision, being, sensation, thought, cannot be long exercised without repose. This repose is in a great measure dependent on their double character. When one organ is weary, the other can be used; as, when the right arm fails, we use the left.

By these periods of action and repose, this life is essentially different from the other: the dull monotony of ceaseless action is relieved. By this means we are enabled to compare one state with the other; and, as comparison is the first step of progress, to this seemingly unimportant fact our progress from infancy is referable. By it the cry of the infant is developed into the speech of manhood, and its crude thoughts ripened into maturity,—results referable to constant action broken by rest.

The organic functions never improve. They are as perfect at infancy as at manhood. Although the size of these organs increases, there is no progress in their offices. They are closely related to the undeviating actions of the inorganic or mineral world. In fact the offices of excretion and secretion can be performed by mineral membranes, equally well as by living tissue; and digestion, the most mysterious of all vital functions, takes place in the test-glass of the chemist as well as in the living stomach; and even tissue, held to be entirely dependent for its formation on living bodies, has not only been created by the chemist, but the mineral elements have been compelled to unite by means of electric currents, and from the compounds thus produced tissue has been created identical with those of living beings.

In this vast and unexplored field, we find our existence going down to the basis of all existence, *the mineral realm;* and our proud natures acknowledge the supremacy of purely inorganic laws, which arise and permeate the domain of life, the mysterious laws of which, to the borders of its spiritual province, apparently are but modifications of those ruling the inorganic world.

When we study the structure of our body, we at once see that all its functions are strictly like those of animals. The blood flows in our veins by the same law,—by a similar combination of arteries and veins, heart and lungs, as in all warm-blooded animals. The processes of digestion, assimilation, secretion, &c., are identical. A unity pervades the kingdom of living beings. They are all moulded after one plan, and man is the archetype of that plan,—its perfection.

The reptile has a heart; but it is so imperfect, only half its blood is oxygenated at once. The heart of man is like that of the reptile, only (what we find presaged in the *highest* reptiles by a partially formed membrane) another division is added. Instead of these, his has four chambers; and the thick, turgid blood of the reptile, in his veins, being fully oxygenated, glows with sparkling vermilion, and is qualified to build a body adequate to the manifestation of the highest mentality.

The dolphin has a fin; the seal a rude attempt at an

arm; the lion a claw; the monkey tribe a hand, farther perfected in *man*, and rendered capable of the most varied attainments. Wide as the interval between the fin of the dolphin and the hand of man may appear, yet in elements they are the same. In number of bones and their arrangement they are embryonically identical; one plan is everywhere present. The dolphin's fin, the huge flipper of the whale, the massive foot of the elephant, have the same elements as the hand of the child, only they are relatively differently developed.

Man stands at the head of the *vertebrate* division, and is the highest in the mammalian class. The characteristic of this division is the possession of a back-bone, or vertebral column, which is divided into sections called *vertebræ*, whence is derived *vertebrate*. Throughout the mammalian class, all species have an equal number of vertebræ in their embryonic state. As the different species become matured, the vertebræ unite; and consequently in the adult animal their number varies. Man conforms, in number, with his class. The only modification is in form, by which the pelvic regions, the lumbar vertebræ, are enabled to support the weight of the entire body in the erect posture. The same may be said of the muscles; but they are enlarged in this region to meet the requirements of the erect position of the spine. No new element, however, is added; and, as will be hereafter seen, this peculiarity, through the anthropoid apes, imperceptibly shades into the lower animals. The vertebral column, in its highest form, is a series of flexible bones, so articulated and modified as to meet the demands of their position. There is a wide difference between the vertebrata in this respect, and the other divisions. While the articulata have a *crust* or shell over the entire surface of their bodies, to which the muscles are attached, and by which the internal organs are supported and protected, the vertebrata have an internal skeleton, which is a system of levers, giving form, support, and protection to the softer parts. As the vertebral column is the characteristic of the highest division of life, and in man culminates in that flower of nature, the brain, every thing connected with it assumes interest and importance.

Bone is a living, growing, vascular substance, uniting when fractured. In this it differs from the shells of mollusks and crusts of insects, which are unvascular, and grow by addition of layers to their circumference, and may be cast off when too small, and by exudition others formed. When animals are fed on colored food it will penetrate their bones, and stain them of its peculiar color. A pig fed on food in which madder was mixed was found to have its bones stained dark red. This shows that bones grow, that their substance is slowly removed, and new particles are introduced.

Bones in the embryo are represented in form by a thin, glairy liquid, which slowly changes to cartilage, in which the particles of lime are deposited concentrically around the blood-vessels which penetrate the first *model*, in concentric layers, or, in flat bones, in plates connecting them.

The characteristic vertebral column is made up of pieces or segments, called vertebræ. Variously modified as these appear in different animals, or in the same animal, they are all reducible to one type.

These vertebræ are subject to great variation; so much so as often to obscure the general type. It was but lately that the generalization was wrought out, that all the bones of the vertebral column were directly referable, whatever might be their form, to the primitive form of the vertebra. In the central portions of the body the vertebræ most nearly approach their typical form; and, in either direction, they become modified as the distance increases. Approaching the caudal extremities, all parts but the central mass become gradually obscured until nothing but a shapeless mass of bone, without even a perforation for the spinal cord, remains. In the other direction, the change, although different, is equally great, as is seen in the parietal segment of the skull of man.

Now it is essential that the structure be well understood, for on its modifications depend the countless changes in character we shall observe in the vertebratæ.

In the skull we see the widest departure from this type. The hæmal arch is reduced, and the neural arch is enormously expanded to enclose the brain. The hæmal arch is here converted into jaws, and acquires, with its new functions, the teeth and the accompanying organs.

A great modification occurs also in those vertebræ to which the limbs are attached. The limbs themselves are accessory organs, budding from appropriate vertebræ. Often several, generally three or five, vertebræ unite in one solid mass; the elements of which are, however, plainly perceptible. These form the pelvic bones, and from them the hind limbs are put forth.

In the amphioxus, the spinal column exists in the the same state as in the embryos of higher species: it is but a simple tube of glairy liquid; and obscure fibrous bands are the only indication of its division into segments.

The fibrous bands become cartilage, the central portions remaining undivided. At this stage the skeleton of the sturgeon is arrested. The points of these bands next become converted into bone, as in many fossil fishes. More commonly the next step is attained when the central portion of the spinal cord is divided, the ossification of all the parts being imperfect as in the sharks. But ossification is never complete in fishes, the juncture of the vertebræ being left hollow, so that they unite by concave surfaces, the cavity being filled with a glairy fluid. The flexibility of the bones of fishes can be readily tested, showing their cartilaginous character.

The elements of vertebræ are remarkably modified in the turtles. The row of plates along the back are modified spinal processes; those on the sides, the ribs; while the under half of the shell is the modified breast-bone. Great as this departure appears, it is not so very remarkable; the ribs are consolidated and brought on the outside.

From the amphioxus up to man all gradations are observed, consisting chiefly in the acquisition of limbs. In fishes, the vertebræ unite with concave surfaces. As we arise through the sauroid fishes to the reptiles, their surfaces become flattened, as in mammals; and we find diverging branches. In reptiles they are generally united with a ball and socket, one side of the vertebræ remaining concave, while the other is largely developed into a ball, which, taking its form from the opposite surface, of course, is nicely fitted and adjusted. In mammals they oppose straight surfaces to each other.

The number of vertebræ possessed by different animals greatly varies. It is greatest in serpents; also very great in saurians, from the enormous development of tail. Many monkeys, from the same cause, have a prodigious number. The loss of the caudal appendage, as in the apes, greatly reduces the number. In mammalia, except from this variation, the number remains very constant; the excessively long neck of the giraffe having no greater number than the pig, which can scarcely be said to have any neck. In the former case they are greatly elongated; in the latter, shortened and compressed. Man, too, has the almost constant number, seven, vertebræ in his neck.

We thus see how one primary element, the simple vertebræ, by its countless modifications produces all the diversity of the vertebrated kingdom. A gelatinous tube, it forms the spinal column of the sturgeon; partially ossified, and converted from cartilage to bone, those of the shark and ray; its opposing surfaces, remaining undeveloped, oppose concavities in the fishes and in the lowest of the reptiles; in serpents, they are articulated by the ball and socket joint; the lowest mammalia, the marsupials, also by a ball and socket, showing their ascent from the batrachians, or frogs. In mammals, as in the higher saurians of the fossil world, by square surfaces; a line of jelly in the amphioxus; a tube in the sturgeon; a piece of hollow bone in the tail of the crocodile; a solid mass of bone giving off ribs in the dorsal regions of all mammalia, thus protecting and supporting the vital agencies; giving off the limbs of quadrupeds, or spreading around the brain, plates of bone protecting it from injury, and in front sending out its appendages, previously acting as ribs, to become facial bones, and jaws for the prehension and mastication of food, ever presenting the same primary elements.

By this comparison of the bony case which encloses the spinal cord and brain, we see the intimate structural relation of man to the animal. By the comparison of vascular, or nervous systems, this beautiful unity is constantly developed; but nowhere more beautifully than in the changing adaptation of the limbs.

The limbs are merely appendages to the vertebræ. This is a startling statement when the complex limbs of the higher mammalia, as of man, are considered; but, by tracing their development downwards, we arrive at the rudimental forms where we can see the actual process of transformation.

In the great divisions of life each strives to attain locomotion by means peculiar to itself. They all employ analogous means; but the real nature of the organs thus used is very different. Thus, the limb of a grasshopper, to appearance, is like the limb of an ox or horse, but in reality it is entirely different, as will be shown.

As animals cannot extract nutriment from the soil, as they depend on living beings for nourishment, it is essential to their maintenance that they be provided with proper organs to pursue and capture their prey. Such organs are given most animals; and those which are destitute are furnished with other apparatus by which they attach themselves to floating bodies, or are drifted by currents.

We shall only consider the fore-arm, as it furnishes a perfect illustration of our subject. Its most rudimentary form is found in the lepiodosiren. They are simple-jointed, rod-like members. In the next higher form, the amphioxus, we find these rod-like limbs becoming jointed, and two digital rays formed; and, ascending to the proteus, a still further complication and approximation to mammalia.

There is a type or model preserved throughout the entire vertebrate kingdom which is ever followed. The limb is always composed of the same elements; some of these may be dwarfed, and when the animal is matured, confounded with others; some may be greatly enlarged or changed in form, but all are represented. This model is the most perfectly expressed in the arm and hand of man. From it we will trace the chief departures by which vertebrate animals adapt themselves to the various functions they perform. Lowest of all is the rod-like member of the lepiodosiren, in which there is no apparent differentiation of organs.

In fishes it is necessary that a resisting surface be opposed to the water, like an oar. This cannot be situated at a distance from the body; for then the leverage would be too great, and instantaneous movement, which is required, could not be attained. Hence it is that the humerus and radius and ulna are shortened or almost obliterated, while the carpal bones remain; and the digital, becoming augmented in number by vegetable repetition, become rays for the support of membrane forming fins.

The same object is attained in the feet of aquatic reptiles by their having a web-like membrane spread between the toes of their feet. In the frog, for instance, we see the digital bones greatly elongated, and supporting a thin, tough membrane. As the foot necessarily contracts when brought forward, this membrane folds up; but when thrown backwards the foot expands, and of course this membrane is stretched so as to offer the greatest resisting surface.

In the paddle of the dolphin, whale, and other marine mammalia, the same mechanical objects are attained by the same means. The bones of the arm are shortened and wholly buried in the body of the animal, the digital and carpal bones only remaining on the outside, giving support to the membrane forming the fin.

In bats, the object is to form an animal for flight; and we see this accomplished by the enormous development of the four digital members, and stretching a fine membrane over them; the three remaining, as will be seen, of the ordinary size, and serving other purposes.

In birds, the object is the same as in bats; but it is accomplished by quite different means. The bones of the arm remain unchanged, but the carpal bones are obliterated as well as most of the digital. Generally, however, two or more of the latter remain, and their first joints become greatly enlarged. The thumb bones sometimes become converted into a spur, as in the domestic fowl.

In the deer and most quadrupeds the humerus, ulna, and radius remain unchanged; but the carpal bones become consolidated and elongated, while the digital are confounded in a hoof, or, if remaining separate, are armed with claws.

Throughout the entire series, we perceive the same elements. All conform to a common type; and the changes, when viewed by the clear light of science, are very slight between contiguous species.

These elements are always recognizable. Thus, commencing at the shoulder, we first meet with the shoulder bone, — scapula; joining this, generally, we meet the humerus, it being only in fishes that it remains undeveloped; next the ulna and radius, whose presence can be always seen, though one of them may remain in a rudimentary condition. At the wrist joint are the carpal bones, usually ten in number, forming two rows; but they may be reduced by non-development to any number less, even to one. Next is the metacarpal bones, usually five, but often reduced in the higher vertebrata to four, three, two, or one; whilst in fishes they may be multiplied to twenty or more. Lastly, we find the digital bones, usually five sets, each composed of three or more bones, but which are subject to the same reduction or multiplication as the metacarpal, to which they are attached. On the modification of these bony elements entirely depends the special adaptation of species, enabling them to be used for terrestrial, aquatic, or aerial locomotion; for diving, swimming, tearing, lacerating, seizing; or entering into the refined mechanism which enables the human hand to serve the dictates of intellect with such certainty and accuracy.

Ultimate analysis of the constituents of man's body, and of animals, shows identical results. A myriad compounds, products of decay, spring from the dissolution of his form as well as theirs. Ammonia, Cyanogen, the Prussiates, and their countless combinations, arise from the wreck of his mortality. He assimilates the grains and herbs of the herbivora, and produces flesh like theirs; he assimilates the ready-made flesh of the herbivora, and builds a system like the carnivora. Whether he partake of plant or animal, or mix both with mineral ingredients, he on every hand acknowledges the closest physical relations with the *lower* animal world. It is absurd and childish to deny this relationship, which science every day makes more complete. No reasoning can be sound unless it keeps this truth clearly in view, and hence the diverse races of men may not have originated from a single pair; but unity of type they all display points to a common source. Nowhere can lines of demarcation be clearly drawn, so imperceptibly do the families of mankind blend at their circumferences. The various classifications which have been attempted are so many proofs of unity of origin; and their confliction shows the fallacy of the theory of diversity. There are no race marks which are reliable; and those thought permanent, undoubtedly are so only by the *equilibrium* established between man and his externals, of which they are the expression.

Buffon makes six varieties of mankind; viz.,—Polar Negro, Tartar, American, Australian, Asiatic, European. Kant divides man into four varieties, white, black, copper, and olive; Hunter, into seven varieties; Netzau, into two; Virey, into three; Blumenbach, into five; Desmoulins, into sixteen *species;* Bury de St. Vincent, into fifteen; Morton, into twenty-two families; Pickering, into eleven *races;* Burke, into sixty-three; Jacquinnot, into three species of one genus. Such are the disagreements of those who have devoted themselves to this study. Granting that mankind are classified by any of these systems, I cannot see how knowledge is advanced. We cannot admit that mankind can have diversity of origin, while so united by one great plan. If a species or variety of the genus Homo sprang up in Europe, and another in America, by agency of conditions existing in those localities, it would be beyond probability that they should both be formed on the same plan: what then of the possibility of sixty-three or more species being formed on the same model? Deny we may, with plausibility, the origin of the diverse races from a single pair six thousand years ago; but the bond of union which exists between them points to a common source.

I see no necessity of obscuring this subject with a tedious classification, and shall introduce none. The classification adopted in the following description of races of men is one founded on the study of languages, and is similar in results to the classification of animals by embryology, or, in other words, by parentage. Each great wave of peoples is thrown together, so that we reduce the divisions to the simplest terms, and discard color, form, and all the accidental effects of conditions.

This classification is thus presented: —

Oriental Negro — Australian, &c.

African — The Caffres and Hottentots. The peoples of Africa south of the Mountains of the Moon.

Semites — Hebrews, Arabians, Armenians.

Turanians — American Indians, the innumerable peoples of North-Eastern Asia, and a great portion of the peoples of Hindostan.

Aryans — The peoples of Europe, the ruling race of Hindostan, and many scattered nationalities.

This classification is presented fully in the accompanying ethnological chart, and accompanying explanation.

I said color and the effects of accidents in this classification are disregarded. If it be examined, we shall find that there are people classed with Turanians that have pure Aryan features and light complexion; and there are those classed with Aryans — the class pre-eminently white — as dark as the lightest Africans. The lines of this classification strike directly across the distinctions which have been considered eminently characteristic. This may appear fatal to this system; but it is found on closest inspection that language, the expression of the mind, is less influenced by conditions than the physical form; and while the latter is greatly modified, the fundamental structure of speech remains unchanged. So far as history furnishes aid it is gladly received; but the period over which it extends is so limited, in comparison with the ages of man's advance which precedes it, that it yields but little light. Reliance must be placed in the perfection of philological research, the results of which will be given in the following pages.

The problem we are to discuss will involve the investigation of the origin, science, and relations of language; the geographical distribution of races; the relation of man to physical conditions; a survey of the races of men; and an inquiry into the causes of deviation.

CHAPTER I.

ANTIQUITY OF MAN.

Traditionary Chronology. — Effects of Prejudice. — Fossil Man. — Imperfection of the Geological Record. — The Plan of Nature is to destroy the Products of Life. — Fossil Human Remains in the New World. — New-Orleans Skeleton, its Age calculated at 27,600 years. — Natchez Skeleton. — Human Fossils in Brazil. — Mounds of the Ohio. — In the Old World. — In the Loess of the Rhine. — In the Maastricht and Hocht Canal. — Arrow-heads of the Valley of the Somme and Seine, of England. — Caverns. — Determination of Age of Bones by Amount of Organic Matter they contain. — Cave of Durfurt. — Caves in France. — Caves of Sailenreuth, Coppingen, Kustritz; of Gower, of North Sicily. — Lake Dwellings. — Danish Seat. — Danish Shell Mounds. — Södertelzo Fossils, calculated Age 16,000 years. — Calculated Age of Arrow-heads in Peat of the Valley of the Somme 120,000 years. — Antiquity of Egyptian Civilization. — Fossil Remains of the Dog. — The Grotto of Sartel. — Summary.

The theological system supported by Christendom maintains that man was introduced on the globe about six thousand years ago by a direct miracle. However derived, this belief has excited a baneful influence on the progress of geology, and the science of history. It makes a wide difference in our views whether we regard man as a once perfect and fallen being, or a savage progressing to perfection; whether he was *created* sixty centuries ago, or has developed from the lowest state through myriads of ages. This pre-conceived opinion, founded on infallibility and revelation, has stood directly in the way of geological discovery in pushing the antiquity of man beyond its dictum. Without this mythological prejudice, the date of man's origin would never have been placed at so recent a period; and with it, scientific men thrust aside the most conclusive evidence with a sneer. Cuvier pronounced the most decided fossil human bones recent; and Buckland, to vindicate his theology, concluded that human remains found beneath those of numerous extinct animals belonged to historic time.

More than half a century ago fossils were discovered, which, had they belonged to any other animal, would have at once, and beyond doubt, placed that animal's origin back to the strata in which they were interred; but, belonging to man, and overthrowing existing chronological dates, they went for nothing. Slowly and patiently scientists have labored; and now a mass of facts are presented which challenge refutation. The most thorough scientific men of the world accept these facts, regardless of the voice of theology. We are receiving, for the first time, positive knowledge. We have lost the given date of man's advent; but we have ascertained that years are nothing when dealing with periods only expressed by *eons* or myriads of millions. We can only learn the order of events: their date is nothing.

An unconquerable prejudice has existed against the discovery of fossil man. I have mentioned and need not enlarge on its cause. Fossil man destroys chronological dates, man's fall; and then why, if not fallen, needs he redemption?

Considering the determination to ignore such discoveries, a very great progress has been made in accumulation of material. It is true they are in many cases not as explicit as might be wished; but, as a whole, they furnish a mass of evidence which cannot be gainsaid. A few years will fill this gap in paleontology, and geology and natural history will perfectly join. It is not strange that so few fossil human remains have been brought to light. Compared with the vast dimensions of the earth's crust, a fossil is a small affair. If we assume the existence of an animal, say the dog, at any geological era taken at random, it is a thousand times more probable that that animal existed in that era than that its remains will be discovered. In localities where they are known to exist, they are rarely met with. The reports of experienced dredgers show that, although they explore the bottom of the sea for hundreds of miles near shores peopled with millions of inhabitants, and in the route of countless sails, works of art are rarely found, and human remains, almost never.

When the Harlem Lake was drained in 1853, in digging the great canal, and thousands of miles of ditches, although it had been a thoroughfare for vessels, and a dense population had dwelt on its shores for ages, only a few coins and the wrecks of two Spanish ships were discovered; not a vestige of human remains.

Nowhere should negative evidence be accepted with greater caution than in geology. Dr. Schmerling, after having found flint tools in forty-two Belgian caves, only found human bones in three or four. Not till 1855 was the first skull of the musk-buffalo discovered. Birds were, until recently, supposed to belong exclusively to the tertiary; and very lately mammalia were supposed to descend only to the oölite. It is not the plan of nature to preserve the products of life. The activity of the forces of decay are brought in play before the cessation of life; and the organism melts into the air, or is devoured by other beings. Not a particle is lost. Were it otherwise, the earth would soon become so encumbered with the rubbish that living forms could not flourish. The preservation of an inanimate organism withdraws, for the time, elements needed in the construction of other organisms; and were not these elements restored as well as withdrawn they would soon be tightly locked in worthless fossils, and the earth, the ocean, and the atmosphere, rendered incapable of supporting life. Thus are the forces of destruction made active; and the tree, the bone, the tooth, the hardest as well as the softest parts, are soon absorbed. Their preservation is the exception where some peculiar circumstances have, as it were, embalmed them.

Now, when a thousand millions of men inhabit the earth, a number equal to which die every thirty years, how few remains are to be found! The bones from Grecian and Roman times, — where are they? Egypt has preserved a comparatively few in her mummies; where are those left to the natural chances of preservation? The bones of the mound-builders, a recent people, are rarely so well preserved as to retain their form, but fall to dust on exposure to the air. Of the herds of bison and deer; of carnivora, as bear, panther, wolves, foxes, which so recently inhabited the forests of this country; with their Indian companions, all of which for countless generations left their bones in the forest soil, — where are their remains? The tooth of time has gnawed them to dust; and they have ascended through plants to form again in the living systems of ox, horse, and man.

Only occasionally, during freshets, or by accidental causes, have rivers borne down on their turbid currents the bloated carcasess of animals, and covered them in silt at their mouths. It is beneath the waters of lake, or ocean, or miry peat bogs, that fossils are preserved; rarely or never on dry land, where they are so exposed that a few years suffices to destroy them. As since the advent of man there has not probably been any material difference in the relations of land and water, and it is beneath the water that organic remains are to be found, we should not be surprised that the geological record of early human history is so meagre. In those places where bones are preserved on land, as caves and peat-bogs, small as the chances are in favor of their fossilization, many interesting discoveries have been made by indefatigable explorers. I shall allude first to those instances where fossil human remains have been found in the New World, as they invariably indicate a more recent origin than those of the Old.

The skeleton found at New Orleans was sixteen feet below the surface, and lay directly beneath the roots of a cypress tree; there being four fossil cypress fôrests above it. To arrive at an approximation to its age, we must study the formation in which it is found. The cypress grows in the low lands bordering the Mississippi. It attains a great size and age. Humboldt supposes one growing in the garden of Chapultepec as at least six thousand years old. If only one generation of trees were produced in each fossil forest which reposes above this skeleton, and the duration of each be taken as six thousand years, then twenty-four thousand years must have elapsed since its interment. But to this duration must be added the time of elevation and depression of each beneath the surface of the Gulf of Mexico, a period for the computation of which we have no data. If we take the estimate of Lyell, of two and a half feet in a century, as the mean of elevation as observed in existing continental movements, and place the necessary elevation and depression of each forest at its minimum of fifteen feet, then the lapse of time between each forest would be twelve hundred years, or thirty-six hundred years for the three intervals, or twenty-seven thousand six hundred years in all, to which must be added the duration of the last or present period. The discovery of the Natchez fossil human bone, of which much has been said, was not attended with sufficient accuracy of observation to give it any importance as evidence of man's antiquity. If, however, its claims be allowed, it is recent when compared to the human fossil remains of Denmark, or the gravel beds of the Somme.

Dr. Lund has discovered in Brazil, in eight different caverns, human remains, all of which bore marks of contemporaneous deposition with the bones of forty-four species of extinct animals with which they were associated.

In a cave on the borders of a lake named Lago Santa, he found human bones mingled with the bones of many extinct animals, moulded together, and consolidated into a very hard breccia. Among the extinct fossil animal remains were those of the ape and horse. It would be an extremely interesting study to investigate the causes which extinguished the horse from this continent. The wild horse of South America is a descendant from Spanish stock, but thrives well from Patagonia to the Great Lakes; and it is difficult to say why it perished.

In South America, near Lima, eighty-five feet above the sea, cotton thread, and plaited rush, and a head of Indian corn were found embedded with recent shells in limestone. At a contiguous point evidence was elicited, that, since the peopling of the country by the Peruvian race, at least this considerable elevation has taken place. This affords no certain data on which a calculation can be based, as the coast often in a single day is elevated several feet, and then perhaps for centuries remains at rest. Taking the foregoing estimate of two and a half feet in a century, eighty-five feet represent three thousand four hundred years as the lapse of time since the threads and plaited straw found a lodgment in the forming limestone. How long previously the Peruvian race occupied the table-lands of the Andes cannot be told.

The mounds of the Valley of the Ohio are of unknown age. They probably were the work of the same race which had begun the incipient civilization in Mexico so ruthlessly destroyed by the Spaniards. For a savage people to migrate across this continent, — their traditions referred their origin to the north, and they were undoubtedly from Asia, — and to advance to so high a degree of civilization, pre-supposes at least several thousand years.

Probably to them, or to the later Indian race, is due the extinction of the mastodon of North, and the gigantic sloths known as the Margatherium, and Mylodon, of South America. The horse, so far from being used by them, was probably extirpated with those huge beings. We here have a key by which to account for the anomalous disappearance in recent times of those animals, the bones of which extend into the human period.

It is, however, in the Old World that the records of vast and incomprehensible antiquity are met with.

So early as 1823, a human skeleton was disinterred by M. Ami Boúe from ancient, undisturbed loess of the Rhine, at Lahr, nearly opposite Strasburg. This loess is the ancient alluvium thrown down by the turbid water of the rivers from the Alps. Previous to its denudation, a thickness of at least eighty feet existed above the skeleton. Nearly half the bones were obtained. They did not lie as if part of a corpse that had been buried there. The fossils were presented to Cuvier, who pronounced them at once to be human; but, pre-occupied by theological chronology, he referred them summarily to recent date.

On excavating a canal from Maastricht to Hocht, in 1815–1823, in the loess, there twenty feet thick, extraordinary numbers of fossils of elephants of the ox tribe, horns of deer, and other mammalia were found. Mingled with these, at a depth of nineteen feet, where the loess reposes on the underlying gravel, in a stratum of sandy loam, overlaid by gravelly and sandy beds, a human jaw with teeth was found. The animal fossils were much more plentiful at the bottom of the loess, but were partially diffused to the surface. This statement of Prof. Crabay is indorsed by Lyell, who, after visiting the locality, "could see no reason for supposing the human jaw to belong to a different geological period from that of the extinct elephant."

The geological evidence of the vast antiquity of man furnished by the Valley of the Somme is, perhaps, among the most conclusive. In the thick stratum of alluvial gravel bordering the river, flint implements have been found at several places, and in great numbers at Abbeville, Amiens, and St. Achuel. They are arrow and spear heads, knives and hatchets, some of which have their edges broken, as though used before they were lost. They are embedded from ten to twenty feet in the solid, undisturbed gravel, and are associated with bones of the elephas primigenius, rhinoceros, horse, deer, hyena, felis spelala, &c., which inhabited Europe at that period. The disappearance of these huge quadrupeds may be as much referable to the agency of man as of climate.

Similar flint instruments have been discovered in the alluvial gravel of the Seine, in the environs of Paris, twenty feet below the surface, accompanied by like organic remains, as well as in the Valley of the Oise.

In England, they have been found in several places in the Valley of the Thames; at Bedford in the Valley of the Ouse, in gravel; at Hoxen in Suffolk; at Icklingham, in which localities they occur from ten to twenty feet below the surface.

The discovery of human bones in caverns, the most probable place for their occurrence, is very significant. It is the locality above all others where we should expect to find the remains of a savage people. Caves are the natural shelter for savage man. There he has left a dim hieroglyph of his existence. Sometimes, perhaps, he expelled the bear and hyena from their dens, or in turn was expelled, or fell a victim to their rapacity, leaving naught but the gnawed fragments of his bones to tell of his existence.

The idea of determining the age of fossils by the amount of animal matter which they contain is incorrect, for, after a time, — and it is of no great comparative duration,— all bones arrive at the same condition by the loss of their organic atoms. There is no situation, in which fossils are found, which can more than temporarily retard this destruction.

The Cave of Durfurt, in the Jura, is situated in a calcareous mountain, and is entered by a shaft twenty feet deep. Here were found the bones of the rhinoceros, bear, hyena, and numerous other extinct animals, and, mingled with them, human bones and pottery. They were embedded in mud and fragments of limestone, in some places to the depth of thirty feet.

There are a great many caves in France that have yielded bones. They have been ably described by Dr. Schmerling. In the Cave of Engihoul the human bones were mixed with those of extinct animals, and were like them in all respects. Near them were found fragments of ancient urns, and vases of clay, teeth of dogs and foxes, pierced with holes to serve the purpose of beads.

In all these caves, as well as those of Belgium, situated as they are in the deepest and most inaccessible localities, buried beneath thick deposits of stalagmite and mud, human bones have been found mingled with those of the extinct elephant and rhinoceros.

They are often found mixed, in a fragmentary breccia, with the bones of these animals, in all instances having precisely the same appearance as the bones with which they are associated.

The Cave of Sailenreuth, in Franconia, is three hundred feet above the river; those of Zahnlock and Kühlock are similarly located, and the cave of Coppingen in the Suabian Alps is two thousand five hundred feet above the sea: those of Kustritz in Upper Saxony are also very elevated. These instances are interesting, because in all of these human bones occur mixed with those of the usual extinct animals, sometimes covered with a *drift deposit* twenty feet in thickness. In some of these caves the human bones were found eight feet below those of the rhinoceros, and in such quantities as to represent man from infancy to maturity.

In the Cave of Gower, South Wales, a fact has been brought to light, which is of a most conclusive character. In the same undisturbed deposit which covers the floor of the cavern, the remains of two species of rhinoceros, and two flint knives were found. Since the occupation of the cavern, the land has subsided beneath the sea; and a deposit of sand has taken place over its floor. How vast the interval required to depress the land beneath the sea, allow a long period for the deposition of sand, and its equally slow elevation!

There are many ossiferous caves in North Sicily,

in which human remains occur with those of extinct animals. The northern coast of that island presents rocks containing recent species of shells, with broken pottery, elevated to the height of three hundred feet. If we allow one hundred feet for the depth of water in which the shells flourished before elevation began, then, at the rate of two and a half feet in a century, four hundred feet of elevation would give 16,000 years as the age of the pottery. But a much greater period must be stated; for no allowance is here made for the time after the deposit of the pottery, before the elevation began.

Herodotus speaks of a small Thracian tribe, that dwelt in the midst of a mountain lake of Pœonia, building their dwellings on piles driven into the bottom of the lake, and connected to the shore by narrow causeways.

That was B.C. 520 years.

In 1853–1854, in reclaiming a part of the Lake of Zurich, piles were discovered, belonging to just such an ancient village. In dredging, abundant evidence of fishing gear was discovered, as pieces of cord, hooks, stone weights, and canoes, one of which, made out of the trunk of a tree, was fifty feet long. Since the direction of attention to this important subject, piles, fragments, and implements have been found in almost every lake in Switzerland. Some of these villages belong to the age of bronze, some to the age of stone.

The sites first studied were on the Lake of Moosseldorf, near Berne. All the instruments found were of stone or bone: the flint employed came from the

South of France, but, from the chippings found, must have been worked up on the spot. The other implements were of jade,—of a kind not found in Europe, and which is supposed to come from the East,—and amber which probably came from the Baltic; facts which show that these savage tribes carried on a widely extended commerce. The Indian tribes of America had arrived at quite as extensive exchanges, the nations on the Atlantic trading as far west as the great lakes of Erie and Huron, and probably the Mississippi.

In the Lake of Constance, at the site of another lake dwelling, arrow-heads of quartz; hatchets of green stone and serpentine; a kind of plated cloth; lumps of carbonized wheat and barley; flat cakes of bread; carbonized apples and pears, such as grow now in the Swiss forests; bones of the ox, sheep, and goat,—have been discovered.

Near Morges, on the Lake of Geneva, is the site of a village of the bronze period. No less than forty bronze hatchets have been there dredged up in a wonderful state of preservation.

The presence of the cultivated cereals, as well as the near approach to the present type of the country made by the solitary skull discovered, renders the remote antiquity of these lake-dwellings uncertain. They undoubtedly are of great age, but modern compared to the flints of the Danish peat.

Numerous examples of artificial islands have been discovered in Ireland; but they have been too uncritically examined: all that is known of them points to the remotest antiquity. They belong to the stone age.

These primitive people dwelt south as well as north of the Alps after the retreat of the great glaciers; for, in Northern Italian lakes, their remains have been recently discovered. Considering that scarcely ten years have elapsed since attention was first called to this subject, a wonderful mass of facts bearing on the age of man have been recorded; but there is a wide field yet unexplored, in which a rich harvest is certain.

The untiring labors of a few zealous Danish geologists have yielded a strong mass of evidence. They have had good material, and have used it well. Nowhere has the remoteness of man's creation been so forcibly shown as in the analysis of their peat-bogs and shell-mounds. At the bottom of the peat, numerous flint and stone instruments occur. Substantially above them, embedded in the peat, is a forest of Scotch fir. This tree has not flourished in Denmark in historic times. After the fir had exhausted the soil, it was succeeded by the sessile oak. This was followed by the pedunculated oak; and, after these forests, came the present beech. Forest trees attain a great age, and it is probable that each of these forests was formed of several generations of trees.

In the time of the Romans, Scandinavia was remarkable for its splendid beech forests; and they still continue to thrive with undiminished vigor. Six thousand years would be the least period which could be assigned for the duration of the present forest; and hence four forests would equal 24,000 years as the age of the flint instruments.

From careful investigation, the Scandinavian antiquarians decided that the remains they discovered should be classified in three epochs: that of stone, the oldest and most savage; of bronze, when man had learned the use of that alloy; and of iron, which is the historic. This classification is at once simple and truthful, and applicable to all remains, in whatever part of the world they are found.

The peat of Denmark is no more remarkable than the immense mounds of shells often met with. Similar ones are to be seen on the Atlantic coast of New England, where the Indians have dwelt for ages, throwing the refuse of their meals together.

These shells belong to living species; but they prove, that, since they were gathered, the geography of the earth has changed. Thus the oyster, periwinkle, and cockle are full sized: but now the Baltic is too fresh for them to flourish, except at its entrance; and, in consequence, they are of diminutive size. Mingled with the shells are fragments of the bones of the wild bull (*aurock*), the roe, deer, lynx, fox, wolf, and dog. The dog is the only domesticated animal the remains of which have been found. It was of small size in the stone age, but larger in the bronze. It became very large in the iron epoch.

The remains of man, of course, would not be found in the refuse heaps, unless these early people were cannibals; but the instruments he used in the chase are common, as flint axes, and arrow-heads. In mounds of contemporary date, where the careful hand of affection consigned them, human skulls have been discovered. These skulls are small and round, with a prominent ridge over the orbits of the eyes, — a mark of inferiority, and extremely large in the chimpanzee. This ancient race were of small stature, and resembled the Lapps.

Skulls of the age of bronze are elongated and larger. These mounds correspond to the older portion of the peat, the canoes found in which show that these little men ventured on the water; and the remains of bones of deep-sea fish in the shell-heaps show that he was not an unskilled mariner.

By careful comparison of the bones of the various ages, venison appears to have been the principal food of the hunter, or stone age; and the flesh of the ox and sheep, that of the bronze, at which latter period the tame pig displaces the wild boar. At the beginning of the age of stone, the goats were the more numerous; at its close, the sheep. The bronze age had two races of cattle, and two of pigs, a horse of medium size, and a small dog. The fox, at first very numerous and serving for food, was at length displaced by the dog. Have we not here a clew to the origin of the dog, the progenitor of which, as is well known, is undiscoverable among living species?

In a section laid open at Södertilge, at a depth of sixty feet, beneath marine strata, the timbers of a wooden hut, with its circle of hearth-stones, and much charcoal, were discovered. In the same strata occur the remains of vessels constructed with wooden pegs.

The strata in which they were found contain the characteristic shells of the brackish waters of the

Bothnian Gulf. As the saltness of the Bothnian Gulf and Baltic depend on the same causes, and as this deposit represents only brackish water, while the oyster and cockle shells of the shell-mounds of Denmark represent water as salt as the ocean, the latter must belong to a period previous to the strata in which the vessels and huts occur.

The time required to sink the land sixty feet, and then slowly elevate it to that height, would suffice to bring us close to that period when Scandinavia was a vast glacier, sending off its erratic blocks far over the site of England. Perhaps by a simple computation we can arrive at an approximation. Scandinavia is undergoing a slight elevation: the process is a continuation of that which has elevated the strata containing the human relics, and converted a large portion of the bed of the Baltic and North Sea into dry land. The area of elevation extends over one thousand miles north and south, and the degree of elevation amounts to five feet in a century at the North Cape, where it attains its maximum, and gradually grows less towards the south, until it reaches zero. It is eight hundred miles from the North Cape to the point where the remains occur; and, consequently, the mean elevation at that point is one foot in a century; so that to produce an elevation of sixty feet would require sixty centuries. But the water must have had some depth when the boats sank, and were enclosed in the ooze. If we assume this at twenty feet, we must add twenty centuries to the above. But this period is only that of depression: that of elevation was equally long, so that for the whole time we have 16,000 years.

This lapse of time is insignificant, if we accept the calculations of M. Boucher de Perthes from data derived from the observed growth of peat. At the bottom of the entire stratum of peat in the Valley of the Somme, thirty feet in thickness, flint tools have been found. Taking the growth of peat at three centimetres, or three-tenths of an inch, it would require for the growth of that peat stratum one hundred and twenty thousand years. More: carrying the antiquity of man still farther into the realms of paleontology, this peat rests on and overlies the drift gravel-beds in which flint tools have been described as being found in the Valley of the Somme! Their age, computed from the thickness of gravel in which they occur, is a vast period; but, when added to that of the overlying peat, it becomes wholly incomprehensible.

On the opposite shore of Sweden, deposits of the same age as those of Sördertilge attain an elevation of even seven hunded feet. The shells found in them are not of the same species as those found in the neighboring sea, but like those several degrees farther north. The climate of Scandinavia was decidedly more arctic then than now. Lyell, by assuming an average elevation of two and half feet in a century, estimates that the present elevation of the coast of Sweden required twenty-seven thousand five hundred years, and this without making allowance for pauses of indefinite duration, which always occur during long-continued elevations or depressions. As the distance from the point of greatest elevation is about the same as Södertilge, one foot in a century would be a mean elevation probably nearer the truth, and yields seventy thousand years as the result.

Vessels have been found in England, buried in the now-deserted channel of the Rother in Sussex, of the Mersey, and the Thames.

In almost all parts of the kingdom, canoes and stone hatchets have been found at considerable depths beneath the surface.

In America, flint arrows and stone hatchets are often turned up by the plough; but they are invariably met with at the *surface*. There has not yet transpired a single instance where they have been so deeply buried as to yield to calculations, results like those of the old world.

Ancient as are the Pyramids, they rest on a deposit yielding evidence of an almost fathomless antiquity. From the stupenduous researches of Hekekyan Bey, made by a series of shafts and artesian borings across the Valley of the Nile, we learn, that when the depth of sixty feet, or the level of the Mediterranean, was reached, fragments of pottery were brought up; and, in a boring by Linaut Bey, fragments of red brick were brought from a depth of seventy-two feet. M. Rosière, in his great work on Egypt, from personal observation, estimates that the deposit made by the overflow of the Nile, which has buried these works of art to their present depth, averages two inches and eighty-eight thousandths in a century. Twenty-two feet would consequently represent forty-one thousand three hundred years; but the auger brought up fragments from the lowest point reached, and thousands of centuries may be represented in the unknown depth of deposits below.

Fossil remains of the dog have been discovered in many places, and the discovery merits more attention than has been bestowed upon it; for the dog has not only been the companion of man, but is a creature formed by his selection and culture from widely different sources. Hence the discovery of its fossils in a given era is almost equivalent to finding the bones of man himself in that era. The antiquity of the faithful instincts of the dog is touchingly shown in a cave of the Canary Islands, where the skeleton of a Guanches is accompanied by that of a gigantic dog, lying as if watching the slumbers of his master.

The similarity of the skeleton of the dog and wolf has undoubtedly led to pronouncing many fossils as of the wolf which belonged to the dog.

Bones of the dog have been found in the caves of Lagoa-Santo in Brazil. They belonged to a variety larger than now living. They were mingled with bones of the huge extinct mammalia of that country, like that found at the foot of the Pyrenees in a stratum of marl, surmounted by compact limestone: it was also associated with the fossil bones of a monkey. This is the more notable, as fossil monkeys are more rare than fossil man. The latter was associated with the rhinoceros, anoplotherium, deer, and antelope.

Several fossils of the dog have been described by Dr. Schmerling. They differ essentially from the wolf or fox, and belong to two well-marked varieties. They were found in a cavern deposit, mingled with bones of bears, hyenas, and other extinct animals.

Of the fossil bones of the genus *Canis*, found in the Cave of Gailenreuth, Cuvier remarked, that they resembled those of the dog much more than those of the wolf. They were mingled in the same deposit with bones of the hyena, tiger, &c., and had the same appearance and consistence, and were evidently of the same age.

A fossil dog resembling the bull-dog occurs in the bone-caverns of England.

The fossils of four types of the dog have been discovered; the immense Canary, pointer, hound, and bull-dog. A smaller variety resembling the turnspit, and that discovered by Mantel in New Zealand, associated with the bones of the *dinornis*, are yet undetermined.

When the pointer set for game, and the hound bayed in the woods of Europe; when the bull-dog growled at the caverns mouth, and the canary watched in its cave, — can we doubt that man was with them, on whom their very existence depends?

A more startling fact remains for statement, one which has received the sanction of that cautious observer, Lyell. In 1852, a grotto was discovered in the face of a cleft forty-five feet high. The entrance was concealed by rubbish; but on systematic exploration, made by M. Lartet, in 1860, beside the seventeen skeletons at first removed, he made other and most wonderful discoveries. It appears that the grotto was the burial-place of an ancient people. After clearing the rubbish away, a slab of stone shut the entrance. In front of this door was a layer seven inches in thickness of ashes and cinders, remains of fires where the friends cooked and ate the funeral feast; the remnants of which, the charred and gnawed bones, were plentifully scattered through the ashes. These bones belonged to the cave-bear, cave-hyena, fox, brown bear, badger, polecat, cave-lion, wild-cat, horse, stag, gigantic Irish roebuck, and aurochs. None of the denizens of their forest came amiss to the voracious appetite of these early people. The larger bones were invariably split for extraction of the marrow, and many of them are more or less burned. The softer and spongy parts were gnawed by hyenas, or other animals, which prowled about the place after the departure of the mourners.

There were a great variety of flint articles, knives, projectiles, sling-stones, chips, and the flint stone from which they were broken, with the round stone used in breaking them out, and bone arrows. Some of the bones were steaked by the flint knives used to scrape off the flesh. No human bones occurred outside of the stone door.

They were not cannibals. Inside were as many as seventeen skeletons. They belonged to a race of small stature. A flint knife, a few teeth of the cave-lion, tusks of the wild boar, and a tooth of the cave-bear carved into a resemblance of the head of a bird, and the bones of the cave-bear, accompanied the skeletons. They were probably amulets, or tokens of the chase. The bears appear to have been placed in the cave entire, undoubtedly to serve as food for the departed on their journey to the land of spirits.

In the gravel-pits of the Somme, the Thames, the Oise, in the peat and shell-mounds of Denmark, we meet the remains of art, associated with the extinct rhinoceros, mammoth, and elephant, showing that, when Europe was a warmer climate than now, and was peopled by the cave-bear, lion, tiger, rhinoceros, &c., man had already reached a rude state of civilization. Here in this grotto, at the foot of the Pyrenees, we find him occupying the position of a conqueror. Judging from the works of art, the remains in this cave are of equal antiquity with the flint arrows and hatchets of the Somme, or the shell-mounds of Denmark. Rough calculation fixes their age at several score thousands of years; yet we find him in a comparatively high estate. He is acknowledged lord of the animal world; the huge cave-bear falls by his arrow; the unwieldy mammoth is sacrificed; the fleetness of the enormous Irish elk does not save it, nor the fierceness of the cave tiger or lion. He provides a sepulchre for the body of the dead; the tribe gathers, and places the corpse of their friend in the prepared grotto; they place by its side the carcass of a bear to sustain the spirit on its long journey, and a flint arrow with which to pursue the cave-lion in that far clime. Then they prepare the flesh of mammoth, or other denizen of the wild, by the funeral fire; partake of the feast: the door is replaced, and the friends depart. Wonderful fact! we find the belief in immortal existence buried among the wrecks of animate forms fossilized in stone. It has survived the gigantic beings of the world of its birth. Mammoths have perished; the cave-bear, lion, and tiger are no more; the rhinoceros, diminutive in size, has withdrawn to Asia and Africa;

the entire fauna and flora of Europe have undergone two great fluctuations; yet the belief in immortal existence after death has grown brighter and clearer, and draws, as to a centre, more and more the activity of mankind.

Were the evidences adduced applicable to any other fossil, they would be considered as incontrovertibly fixing its situation in the drift.

It will be seen that all calculations on the period of man's advent, in years or thousands of years, necessarily are but rough approximations. Science can here deal only with the order of events. All that geology contends for is the removal of his advent from historic times to the first age of the past, — the drift. If his birth dates in that age, there is no difficulty in accounting for the great varieties of race, and his dispersal over the whole earth; for the continental masses were not then related to each other as at present. The Atlantic Ocean was then in a great measure continental, or had large islands studding its expanse. The weald of England indicates an indefinite stretch of land to the west or south-west, it being the estuary and delta of a large river flowing from that direction. There are reasons for supposing that this tract did not subside, and the Atlantic take its present form, until a recent geological date; and that the Old and New Worlds were in communication across the present site of the Atlantic by means of projecting continental masses. Asia, on the other side, approaches so near, that there is a free intercommunication between the Esquimaux tribes across Behring's Straits.

The facts furnished by geology extend the advent of man so far into the night of time, that the Pyramids, and ruins of ancient cities, even the rude stone columns of Stone-Henge, are of yesterday. All of these show a highly civilized state. In their day, man was acquainted with the metals, the principles of refined architecture, the art of writing, the measurement of time, and had acquired the social amenities of refined nationality; but what shall we say of man of the drift? A rude and colossal world spread around him; in the midst of a dense wilderness inhabited by savage and colossal beasts, we first find him, armed only with a flint arrow. How long he had existed previously, we as yet cannot tell; but he had advanced from a ruder estate by a process slow and painful. Progress is in a geometrical ratio. The more enlightened a nation is, the greater will be the rapidity of progress. Savage tribes remain from age to age apparently without change. The study of his progress from the age of stone to that of bronze illustrates the slowness of his advance. Bronze presupposes the knowledge of two metals, copper and tin. The first exists often in a pure or native state; the latter is not only rare, but its extraction from its ore requires a considerable knowledge of chemistry. The proportion of each required to produce the hardest bronze might be learned by experiment. After all this knowledge had been acquired, the instruments made from it were cast after the fashion of those of stone. The bronze hatchet was fashioned just like the stone. It is considerably higher up in the strata in which they occur, corresponding to a long elapse of time, before the savage learns that he can, with the more plastic material, improve the form of his hatchet and arrow-head by departing from the form of those of stone.

From the age of stone he passes to that of bronze. He at first has no domestic animals; but we see how, in the preceding pages, he acquired the dog, sheep, ox, pig, and goat. These acquisitions were not made in a few centuries. The American Indian has inhabited this continent from immemorial time; yet the only domestic animal he has acquired is the dog,—a kind of mongrel wolf. How long before he would have tamed the bison or the deer? The ancient man of Europe had the aurochs, as wild and fierce as the bison, to subdue, and the wild, goat-like mountain sheep, as fleet as the deer, to domesticate. He had learned to manage the horse, and wrought a great departure in the pig from its parent, the savage wild boar. All this he had done while he still possessed only a bronze hatchet and arrow. But even with these he had extirpated the mammoth and elephas *primigenius*, and by the power of intellect taken the commanding position he has since held over the animal world. All of this vast duration lies far below the seventy-two feet of Nile deposit, which, as we have said, represents twelve hundred centuries; and this underlies the base of the hoary Pyramids, which of themselves are scarcely of historic time, reaching back, according to Lepsius' calculations, to within one hundred and twelve years of the creation, according to received chronology.

Perhaps these immense periods already bewilder the

understanding; but we must add, that below all these combined periods of savage life, of twelve hundred centuries of Nile deposit and the Pyramids, lies a stretch of ages during which man existed, adown which we gaze into night with our senses perfectly appalled. We have stated that human remains have been discovered in the Alps twenty-five hundred feet above the sea, and covered with a deposit of drift. The arrow-heads described also belong to the drift. All facts prove that man inhabited the earth during that period. When it covered Europe with ice and snow, man could not have been introduced: he must have previously inhabited that country, as every circumstance would debar his approach to its inhospitable shores while it continued; hence man must have first appeared in the later tertiary, and already become established before the drift began. We thus place the entire drift, or pleistocene period, between the present and the origin of man. The continuance of that period cannot be measured by years; but an idea can be obtained by comparing it with other periods. After careful inspection of the weald of England, Darwin estimates the time required to effect its observed degradation at 306,662,400 years. The degradation effected by the drift was equally great as that of the weald. There was time enough to cover the northern hemisphere to the 38° latitude, and in many places lower, with an icy sea covered with icebergs, and to wrap the land in vast glaciers, and to allow the degradation thus begun to continue until not an exposed rock or mountain-peak should bear witness of its action. The interval since Niagara began to cut its channel from Ontario, or since the Mississippi flowed in its present channel, are but centuries in this time. Lyell estimates the age of the delta of the Mississippi at 100,000 years; but he makes little allowance for the fine sediment which is more than one-half of that brought down by the river, and on which his calculations are based. This would certainly double the interval. To this must be added the age of the bluffs, also of fluviatile deposit, in many places two hundred and fifty to three hundred feet in height, and probably twice the antiquity of the present delta, or 400,000 years in all. We can thus go on making estimates, all reaching into incomprehensible past time; but we cannot do more than thus approximate by the million or the hundred million, and must, as yet, content ourselves with the order of events.

CHAPTER II.

RELATIONS OF MAN TO THE ANTHROPOID APES.

The Climate of the Tertiary Warm. — Whence came the Savage of the Flint Arrow-head? — Primates, no Break or Chasm between them and Man. — Fossil Primates, Dryopithecus, of the Swiss Jura, Eocene. — Linnæan Classification of PRIMATES. — Embryonic Form of the PRIMATES. — ANTHROPOID, or MAN-LIKE APES. — First Account of the PONGO.— Anatomical Structure. — The GIBBONS. — ORANG-OUTANG. — CHIMPANZEE. — GORILLA. — The Point of Man's Contact with the Animal World, the Quadrumania. — Comparison of Structure of the Hand, Foot, Vertebral Column, Pelvis, Skull, and Teeth. — Brain, Convolutions of. — Correspondence of *Fossil Human Remains*, the Engis Skull, the Neanderthall Skull. — CONCLUSIONS.

THUS far our investigations have been in the sepulcral land of paleontology, where, in mausoleums hewn by the sea, the wreck of human beings and of the animal creation are entombed. Before the icy drift ocean laved the northern continents, wrapped in an almost perpetual and universal coat of ice thousands of feet in thickness, there existed, as has been previously shown, a warm climate. This is not only proved by the bones of elephants and mastodons, — they may have inhabited a comparitively cold climate, —but the contemporaneous presence of the rhinoceros and hippopotamus, the tiger, lion, and hyena, speak of a genial clime extending over Northern Europe and Asia.

It is in this period that we obtain the first traces of man. It is a flint arrow-head, a stone axe, so rudely shaped that we pause before we pronounce them works of art, and throughout this immense elapse of time we only obtain such traces of the rudest existence.

From whence came this savage whom we find even in traditional ages, naked or skin-clad, wandering through the gloomy forests of Europe, often feasting on the bodies of his fallen enemies?

We descend step by step; we pass into the drift, finding there the lowest savage man; leaving whom, and descending into the true tertiary, we meet with fossil primates, the highest group of animals. Few fossils of the latter have been discovered; but, when hundreds have been exhumed and placed side by side in an ascending line, there cannot be the least doubt, that, between the highest *primate* and the lowest savage, there will be no break, no chasm, but a perfect and complete series.

To hazard conjecture in the present state of science is perhaps immature; but there are certain great deductions which may be drawn from received facts, which appear to converge to one irrefragable conclusion. Many scientific writers boldly put forward the views, based entirely on negative evidence, that, by the absence of fossil *primates*, man is completely cut off from the animal world by an impassable chasm. The preposterous assumption of such criticism will become apparent when we consider that scarcely a single living specimen of the ourang or gorilla has been procured. Very little is known by naturalists of the higher *primates*, and still less of their fossil remains. The dense and inaccessible forests of Borneo and Sumatra, Loango and the Gaboon, conceal the orangs, troglodytes niger, and gorilla. The geological provinces of the present correspond in a great measure to those of the tertiary, and hence it is exactly in those inaccessible countries that such fossils must exist. It is by mines and works of engineering that fossils are principally brought to light. Nothing of this kind has broken the soil of those countries. Even to the northward, the only direction they could extend, the country is almost unknown. While undoubtedly many living species remain undescribed, how puerile to found an objection on the absence of fossils!

The most notable fossils yet discovered of primates is that of the DRYOPITHECUS of Lartet, found in the Upper Miocene of Sauson, near the foot of the Pyrenees, in the south of France. It was a long-armed ape or gibbon, about equal to man in stature.

M. Rütsmeyer has discovered, in the eocene of the Swiss Jura, remains of a monkey allied to the lemurs. Europe, the only country where a partial search even can be made, was, according to the high authority of Lyell, too cold during the pliocene, or latter tertiary, for monkeys.

It is not my purpose to array the brute in comparison with man; to sink his noble and immortal qualities to the level of the beast. If we admit the unity of type in the animal world, and ignore any other creation than that of law, how can we escape from basing the origin of man on the highest members of the animal world?

The facts on this subject are scanty; but so vital is the importance of the theory to which they refer, that I shall devote a considerable space to their presentation. It has been said, and is constantly repeated, that a break, a chasm, an impassable gulf, exists between even the lowest man and the highest animal, — a gulf nothing but a miraculous creation by God can bridge. Philosophers may reason on either side,— the animal side, or the human; but at this gulf they must pause, and, if conscientious, be brought to a realizing sense of divine interposition, and the helplessness of philosophy.

Now, it is evident that the conclusions drawn from the animal realm agree with those drawn from the domain of man: over the gulf, only an arch is wanting to complete the chain of a perfect system of nature. The arch I am endeavoring to build may be imperfect; but I am confident, rude as it necesssarily must be in the present state of our knowledge, that it may serve as a bridge until material is gathered for a better.

The facts I have gathered I have severely sifted, and their statements as severely condensed, reserving only the essential particulars which bear directly for or against the present theory of the derivation of man.

I do not deny the existence of a chasm. I understand that in the gorilla there is not a single bone, muscle, or fibre, but differs so much from the corresponding part in man, that it can be readily determined. But man does not differ more from them than they differ from each other; a fact brought out boldly in the classification of that master mind, Linnæus. He called the order embracing man, apes, and lemurs, primates. This he divided into seven families: THE ANTHROPINI, containing the various races of men; the CATARRHINI, the Old-World apes; the PLATYRHINI, the New-World apes, except the MARMOSETS; LEMURINI, the lemurs; the CHEIROMYINI; and the GALŒPITHICUS, the flying lemur.

Since his day, man has been set apart in an order by himself; but, by painful research, he is again replaced where the sagacity of the great naturalist assigned him.

I do not desire to make the chasm appear less than it is. It is such a one as exists between all genera, when viewed across the lines of their advance. It is to fossil anthropoids we must look for a perfect series, as they, not the living, are the true progenitors of man. All we claim is, that as we take Greek, Latin, German, and go to Sanskrit, not for their origin, but, because it is an older branch, we can trace their common origin to a parent from which allare derived; so we go to the anthropoids, as to an older branch, to learn of the common parentage of all.

Here an explanation may be inserted, else the gorilla may be considered as a link in the chain of beings, which it is not. The progenitors of both gorilla and man are entombed in the earth. They are divergent lines of advance from such progenitors; as we say that the German and the Hindoo sprang from an early race in Central Asia, not one from the other, and each has advanced after its own manner. It is on this account that analogies are between the lowest types of orders, and not the highest of one and lowest of the next. If we compare, it must be directly across the lines of advance. It is interesting to learn that in its fetal state the embryo partakes of the form of its ancestor more closely than in its adult. Fetal growth depends on hereditary descent; and, before the influence of conditions is exerted on its plastic form, it copies its earliest ancestors. The young lobster is almost a perfect tribolite, a crustacean which lived in the earlier geological ages; the young salmon is a sauroid, a very early form. In the young dog or cat or colt, the distinctions of variety are ignored, the young of all varieties of dog closely resembling each other; and so of cats and horses, sheep, &c. In like manner, the young chimpanzee or gorilla more closely resembles man, and closer still the infant than when matured; and the young of the monkey tribe anticipate remotely and approach to a typical form. In the young gorilla, on the principle that it copies its ancestral form, we see a picture of that early being from which sprang the human line of advance. If future discoveries confirm this inference by bringing to light fossils of as high grade as the young chimpanzee or gorilla, I know not where this reasoning can be broken.

The first notice of the man-like apes was given in 1598 by Pigafetta, in "Description of the Kingdom of Congo," but was so overcharged with fiction that it only creates a smile. In a quaint book published in 1613, entitled "Purchas his Pilgrimage," the apes are introduced with great relish; but the accounts are extravagantly fabulous. In both works, and, in short, in all the writings which relate to this subject, up to the beginning of the present century, the fabulous largely predominates. The abominable caricatures which ornamented their pages are enough to bring contempt on their descriptions. It was not until very recently that accurate portraits or descriptions were obtained. The works of these old authors have nothing worthy of introducing in a present work. Their perusal is exhilarating from the wonder which their subject seems to excite, a wonder reaching perfect credulity, receiving every thing; and the more unreasonable, the better are they pleased.

Linnæus never saw an anthromorphus ape, and his illustrations are childish caricatures. Buffon had the opportunity of examining a young chimpanzee, and an adult gibbon, the first and the last living specimen of that species brought to Europe in many years thereafter.

In his great work in 1766 on natural history, he gave the first correct description of the orang, pongo, and jocko; but, as all these animals then brought to Europe were immature, he supposed that they all belonged to one species, or the great orang. Twenty years afterwards he modified his opinion so as to make two species, a large and a small.

Cuvier classed the pongo as a baboon in his "Règne Animal," but in the second edition of that work considers it as an adult orang. But not until 1835 was a clear and trustworthy account published on the chimpanzee and orang. In this, Prof. Owen for the first time gave correct figures of these animals, and a comparison of their skeletons. The result of all investigations up to the present is the accurate delineation of four species of man-like apes or anthropoids, the gibbon and orang of Eastern Asia, the chimpanzee and gorilla of Western Africa.

The anatomical peculiarities of these may be thus stated: They have the same number of teeth as man, four incisors, two canines, four false molars, and six true molars in each jaw, or thirty-two in all. The number and character of their milk-teeth also agree with man's; they are twenty in number, four incisors, two canines, and four molars, in each jaw. Their nostrils have a narrow partition, and look down, whence their name *catarrhine;* and their arms are longer proportionately than man's. The chimpanzee approaches nearest to man in the length of its arms; and, in the series, the gorillas, gibbons, and orangs follow, the gibbon when standing upright being able to reach the ground with its hands. Their arms are terminated by true hands, and the legs by true feet. The great toe is more flexible than in man, and can be used like a thumb. They are entirely tailless, and are destitute of the cheek-pouches which characterize the monkey. They are exclusively confined to the tropical regions of the Old World; and, from the record of fossil remains, always were thus confined.

It is unnecessary to present a classification of these apes. The classification, if perfect, would be profitless, but is now very far from perfection. I shall give a description of each drawn from accurate sources, rejecting every thing that appears unreliable. Our knowledge is extremely deficient; and it must be confessed that we know almost as little of ther habits as the last century did of their anatomy. They dwell in the most inaccessible regions of the globe to Europeans, and have never been seen in their native haunts by men qualified by science to appreciate and note the essential facts wanted. A Wallace is not found once in a generation qualified to penetrate the jungle of the tropics, and observe and reflect on the new nature there unfolded. We may safely say that one half of the earth is yet unknown to us. The wild stories of ordinary travellers are wholly untrustworthy; and nearly all are too much engaged in telling of their own inconveniences to devote a line to the subjects of vital importance to science.

The gibbons number about a half-dozen species, and dwell in the Asiatic Islands of Java, Sumatra, Borneo, and in Malacca, Siam, Arracan, and, to an unknown extent, in Hindostan. They are the smallest of the anthropoids, being about three feet high when erect. They are of various colors, and, according to Dr. Müller, lovers of the precipitous mountains, although they do not ascend higher than the limits of the fig. Their voice has a tremendous volume, like that of the howling monkeys of South America. It is grave, and may be heard half a league, resembling the sounds goe-ek, goe-ek, goe-ek, goe-ek, goe goek, ha, ha, ha, ha, haaa-ā-ā-ā: when confined to a room, it is deafening. This animal is not more than one-fourth the size of a man; yet the voice of the latter, if as strong, would be audible five or six miles.

All the species of gibbons generally walk erect, and sleep in a sitting posture. Mr. Bennett, in his "Wanderings in New South Wales," says that one in his possession always walked erect, assisting itself with its hands, — as its arms were so long that its fingers reached the ground, — or more usually with its arms uplifted. Their gait is quick, but awkward.

This is the testimony of Drs. Burrough and Lewis. Mr. Martin says, "Pre-eminently qualified for arboreal habits, and displaying among the branches amazing activity, the gibbons are not so awkward or embarrassed on a level surface as might be imagined. They walk erect, with a waddling or unsteady gait, but at a quick pace; the equilibrium of the body requiring to be kept up, either by touching the ground with the knuckles, — first on one side, then on the other, — or by uplifting the arms so as to poise it. As with the chimpanzee, the whole of the narrow, long sole of the foot is placed upon the ground at once, and raised at once, without any elasticity of step."

It cannot be doubted, from all this concurrent testimony, that the gibbon walks erect; but it is at home in the branches of the forest, where it springs from branch to branch as though furnished with wings. It clears spaces of forty feet, leaping from branch to branch for hours at a time without apparent fatigue. They will seize a bird midway of their longest leaps with one hand, and grasp a branch with the other, — a feat never equalled by any circus performer. When going with a velocity scarcely traceable by the eye, they will suddenly seize a branch, and, as if by magic, seat themselves upon it.

They are of gentle disposition unless irritated. Their food is fruits and insects, and they relish animal diet. They have a mental endowment superior to the brute, and a consciousness of right and wrong, if we can believe a reliable observer. Mr. Bennett, who, after speaking of a gibbon who stole a bar of soap, but returned it as soon as he saw that he was discovered, remarks, "There was certainly something more than instinct in that action: he evidently betrayed a consciousness of having done wrong, both by his first and last actions; and what is reason, if that is not an exercise of it?"

Drs. Müller and Schlegel in 1845 published an exhaustive account of the orang-outang. This animal inhabits the low plains of Borneo and Sumatra, and is rare. It loves the densest jungle, where they usually live singly, except at certain seasons. The young are under their mother's care an unusual length of time, and are carried against her breast. It is uncertain how long they are in reaching maturity; but it is probable they do not until ten or fifteen years of age, and that they live to be forty or fifty years old.

The orang has none of the agility of the gibbon. It is sluggish, and only stirs to appease its hunger. It will sit down, its arms drooping beside it, and remain without a motion for hours. During the day it ascends to the loftiest branches, but at night descends. It selects a proper place, where the branches are solid, and makes a bed of twigs and leaves, sometimes several inches thick. The orang rises with the sun, and goes to bed about the time of its setting. He lies on his back, or, for change, on his side, resting his head on his arm for a pillow. On windy, rainy, or cold nights, he contrives to make himself comfortable by wrapping up in several huge palm-leaves, which he uses as blankets.

He has none of the agility of the monkey; and, although he seeks the topmost branches of the largest trees, he is an awkward climber, ascending laboriously exactly as a man would do. He is careful lest he get a fall, never trusting a branch until he has first tested its strength by shaking it: this he will do even when closely pursued. On the ground, he walks on all-fours; but the length of his arms compels him to stand nearly upright, or in the position of an old man. His feet touch the ground only at their outer surface or edge; and the hands touch only at their inner edge, the thumb serving as a strong point of support. When pursued it will run as fast as a man, but can be soon overtaken. It never walks perfectly upright, and all representations of its doing so are incorrect.

Its long arms are serviceable in gathering fruit from branches too slender to support its weight. Its food is exclusively vegetable: blossoms, young leaves, bamboo, figs, and other fruits.

When taken young, he is docile, and seeks human society, but is naturally wild and sly, and, when wounded, will rush on his assailants with a rage and strength which nothing can withstand. Usually he seeks to hide himself, or climbs to the highest branches, uttering a singular cry, at first very high, but subsiding into a low roar. When pursued, he will break off branches, and throw them at his pursuers. Wallace says, "In one case a female, on a durian-tree, kept up for at least ten minutes a continuous shower of branches, and of the heavy spined fruit as large as

32-pounders, which most effectually kept us clear of the tree she was on. She could be seen breaking them off, and throwing them down with every appearance of rage, evidently meaning mischief."

The crocodile is the only animal attacked by the orang; and then the former is the aggressor, watching for the latter as he comes down to drink. The natives say that the orang is more than a match for the scaly monster, tearing at his throat, or beating him to death with stones or clubs.

The character of the orang, given by Müller, is exceeding bad: "He is a very wild beast, of prodigious strength, and false and wicked to the last degree. If any one approached, he rose up slowly with a low growl, fixed his eyes in the direction in which he meant to make his attack, slowly passed his hand between the bars of his cage, and then, extending his long arm, gave a sudden grip, usually at the face." His intelligence was great, his hearing acute, vision less perfect, and his under-lip the organ of touch. When he drank he doubled the latter up like a trough, and turned the water given him into it.

There are several species of orang in Borneo. Their average height is four feet two inches. The color of the hair varies with individuals. Some have the rudiments of a nail on the great toe, others have not. The form of the skull is also subject to great variation, unlike all other wild animals. The length of the muzzle, and slope of the profile, the width and height of the orbit of the eyes, and development of the cranial ridge, vary as much as among European skulls; no two being alike.

The chimpanzee has been often brought to Europe while young; but no one previous to Dr. Savage has described the habits of the adults in their native wilds. It is larger than the orang, measuring five feet in length. It is often seen walking; but, when it finds itself observed, it immediately falls on all-fours, and runs away. When it stands erect, it throws its arms back of its head, or behind its back, to balance itself. Its natural position is on all-fours; but owing to its toes being bent inward so that their upper surface rests on the ground, and its fingers being also much bent, its gait is awkward and shaky. Its home is in the branches of tall trees. It is an expert climber, and, like the gibbon, will throw itself from branch to branch with great agility. They are not gregarious, but families remain together; and, for amusement, large numbers assemble. They are then boisterous and frolicsome; hooting, screeching, and drumming with sticks on hollow trees.

They never make an attack, but, when assailed, will throw their arms around their foe, and draw him up to their formidable teeth. They feed on vegetables; but in a state of domestication, although they refuse it at first, they readily acquire a taste for flesh.

It avoids the abode of man, and builds its nest in the dense forest in a similar manner to the orang.

"They exhibit a remarkable degree of intelligence in their habits, and, on the part of the mother, much affection for their young. In a recent case, the mother, when discovered, remained upon the tree with her offspring, watching intently the movements of the hunter. As he took aim, she motioned with her hand, precisely in the manner of a human being, to have him desist, and go away. When the wound has not proved instantly fatal, they have been known to stop the flow of blood by pressing with the hand upon the part, and, when they did not succeed, to apply leaves and grass. When shot, they give a sudden screech not unlike that of a human being in sudden and acute distress." — *Dr. Savage.*

On the same authority, we have the very full and reliable account of the last of the man-like apes, the gorilla. He shows that the names "Pongo," Euché-eko, Engé-ena, and "Jocko," belong to two or more species to which they have been indiscriminately applied. Its known habitat is Guinea, from the Camaroon to Angola, and how much farther is unknown. It is about five feet high, and disproportionally broad across the shoulders. It is covered thickly with coarse black hair, which becomes gray with age. They walk by thrusting their long arms forward, and then, resting their hands on the ground, give their body a swing between them, like a man walking by the aid of two crutches. When it walks erect, which it inclines to do, it throws its arms upward to preserve its balance.

They live in bands; and usually there is but one male to each band, the strongest male vanquishing or destroying the weaker. Their dwellings are leafy beds made in the convenient crotch of a tree, and are occupied only at night.

They are ferocious, and never run from man. They are objects of greatest dread to the natives. When first observed, the male gives a terrific cry like kh-ah, kh-ah! opening wide his enormous mouth. At the first cry, the females and young conceal themselves. He then rushes towards his assailant. This he does in an erect posture. His mouth is distended, showing his glistening teeth; his under lip hangs down, and the hairy ridge is contracted over his eyes, presenting an aspect of indescribable ferocity, the more from the half-human expression which gleams beneath this brutality. As he rushes on, he strives to terrify his adversary by unearthly shrieks. If the hunter is not sure of his aim, he waits until the gorilla seizes his gun and conveys it to his month; then he fires. If his gun should fail, the barrel is crushed between the jaws of his foe; and the contest is soon fatal.

Having briefly stated the little that is reliably known of the habit of the man-like apes, I shall proceed to an equally brief comparison of structure.

If man belongs to the animal world, he must touch it at some point. The popular classifications of animals teach the relations he sustains. It is not to the dog, the horse, the deer, that he is closest related, but to the quadrumana, or ape family. It is not difficult to make this assignment, nor is it more so to yield the place next to him to the chimpanzee or gorilla. On inquiry, we shall find that the interval which separates the gorilla from man is no greater than that which separates the gorilla from members of its family, or the extreme races of men from each other. The gorilla's brain is smaller, its legs shorter, and its arms, feet, and hands longer, than those of man. But man varies in the proportion of these members, and the species of anthropoids present a wide variation. The hylobate contains within itself the extreme variation of both pairs of limbs; its arms being as much longer than the gorilla's as the latter's are longer than man's, and its legs are as much longer than man's as man's are longer than the gorilla's.

The mandrill's limbs are of nearly equal length, being shorter than the spinal column; and its hand and feet have the same relative size to the spine and to one another as in man. The spider monkey has legs longer than its spine, and arms longer than its legs; the indri [*Lichanotus*] has legs longer than its spinal column, while its arms are little more than half as long. Thus do we see, that, in this striking conformation, the apes differ more from each other than they do from man.

The hand and foot of the PRIMATES, or man-like apes, agree with those of man. It has been said, and the classification of the monkeys as quadrumana is based on the idea, that they have four hands. This is erroneous. The primates have true feet and true hands. To prove this, we need enter into no lengthy anatomical discussion. There are a few salient points which prove the matter conclusively. In the toes, there are first the phalanges, then metatarsal bones, forming the toes as the same do the fingers. As we enter the massive portion of the hand or foot, the relations of the bones change. The tarsus, which corresponds to the carpus of the hand, forms four short polygonal bones in a row. In the foot, instead of four more tarsal bones, there are but three; and these do not lie side by side. One forms the projecting heel; another lies on this on one face, and forms by another, with the bones of the leg, the ankle-joint; while its third face articulates with the remaining tarsus, which unites it to the metatarsus. The greater or less flexibility of the great toe, in the character of a thumb, is of no consequence, as it presupposes no anatomical differences. Thus there is a marked difference between the hand and the foot. If we examine a gorilla, we shall find the same differences. Its foot is set more obliquely, and the great toe is more flexible; but in bone and muscle it is a foot, not as perfect as man's, which must always support the weight of the body in an upright position, but in every sense of the word a true foot.

Man does not depart from the gorilla in hand or foot more than the orang departs from the gorilla; and the lower monkeys depart still more widely. In some the great toe and the thumb become entirely dwarfed, and are concealed under the folds of the skin, as in the spider-monkeys; while in others they are directed forwards, and armed with curved claws like the other digits, as in the marmosets. But, after all these changes, the foot remains essentially a foot in the lowest of the monkeys, and the hand a hand.

The vertebral column of man presents an elegant curve, by which the shoulders are arched, and the back hollowed, and the weight of the body balanced. The gorilla and chimpanzee, especially when young, present the same, though in a less degree. They have the same number of vertebra. The gorilla has thirteen pairs of ribs, while man has but twelve; often, however, he has thirteen pairs. The lower apes greatly vary, departing widely from this number. The pelvic or hip bones are broad and strong in man, in order to support the viscera in an erect posture. The gorilla generally walks erect, and its pelvic bones are much like man's. As the apes are examined, it is found, that, in direct proportion as their habits are to walk upright, the hip bones are stronger; and the opposite, until they become thin blades, in those who never stand erect. Between the pelvis of the gibbons and gorillas there is more difference than between that of the gorilla and man.

The skull of man is comparatively smooth. That of the anthropoids is very ridgy and dense. It is quite different from its external appearance. The low facial angle is not produced by deficiency of skull so much as prominency of the facial bones. It is said that the skull and facial bones widely differ from man's, but not as much as the members of the ape family differ from each other. The proportions of the gorilla's muzzle are enlarged in the baboon, and projected forward in a brute-like manner; while in the former the development is downward,— essentially a human characteristic. The projection of the muzzle of the baboon is carried farther and farther in the monkey's, and becomes essentially like other brutes in the lemur.

In short, wherever the conformation of the skull, the face, or the skeleton, of the man-like apes differs from man's, greater differences can be found between them and the lower members of the ape family.

In the brain, that most important organ of animal life, and which determines by its development the amount of intelligence manifested, the same holds true.

The apes furnish a complete series of gradations of the brain, from the rodents to one little lower than that of man. Nature seems determined to break down all classificatory distinctions between apes and man founded on anatomical structure of that most vital organ. In the whole family, except the lemurs, the posterior lobes of the cerebrum conceal the cerebellum, and the posterior cornu, hippocampus major and minor, are developed. In many (as *chrysothrix*), the posterior lobes extend relatively farther back than in man. This is quite contrary to the received notion, which has been given in the books, that the posterior lobes of the cerebrum of apes were so undeveloped, that, looking down on the brain, the cerebellum was exposed to view. "In fact," writes Prof. Huxley, "all the abundant and trustworthy evidence (consisting of the results of careful investigations of these very questions by skilled anatomists) which we now possess leads to the conviction, that so far from the posterior lobe, the posterior cornu, and the hippocampus minor, being structures peculiar to and characteristic of man, as they have been over and over asserted to be, even after the publication of the clearest demonstrations of the reverse, it is precisely these structures which are the most marked cerebral characteristics common to man and the apes. They are among the most distinct simian peculiarities which the human organism exhibits."

"According to M. Geoffroy, the brain of the young orang bears a close resemblance to that of a child; and the skull also might be taken at an early age for that of the latter, were it not for the development of the bones of the face." The change effected in the adult skull is produced by the excessive growth of the cranial ridges, which serve for the attachment of muscles.

The convolutions of the brains of apes exhibit every stage of advance, from the marmosets, which present an almost smooth surface, to the orang and chimpanzee, which in form and depth fall little below that of man. What is notable and of great weight in determining the unity of man and animals is, that, where the convolutions first appear, they form, as it were, a skeleton map of the brain of man, occupying the same place as in his brain; and, as we arise, at each advance the new convolutions agree with similar ones in his brain, until, in the man-like apes, the constant presence of fissures absent in his brain, the different arrangement of some convolutions, — unessential characters, — is all the difference between their brains and that of man's.

Their brains are not as heavy in proportion to their bodies as man's, and make here a greater departure than in any other direction. The lowest estimate of a healthy European brain cannot be placed lower than thirty-two ounces, nor of a gorilla at more than twenty ounces. But the gorilla is nearly twice as heavy as a European of so small a brain; so that the relation would be as ten ounces to thirty-two, or say only one-third. But European brains have weighed sixty-five ounces, and hence the gorilla would have but two-thirteenths as heavy a brain. This subject of size of brain explains the wide departure of man's intellect from the animal world.

In spinal column, in skull, in teeth, in hand, in foot, or brain, there is no structual variation placing man beyond the animal, or assigning him to another type of structure; but every fact proves the perfect unity of his type of being with theirs.

There is one consideration more, which bears directly on this question: Do the human fossil skulls make any perceptible approach to the gorillas? The interval of time between us and these fossils is very great, but is insignificant compared with the duration since the introduction of man; so that the few mutilated specimens as yet discovered do not belong to a sufficiently early age to show any great approximation, yet they certainly make a step in the direction of the animal, and that beyond the most savage of existing men.

The Engis skull from a cave in the Valley of the Mense, on the authority of Lyell, belonged to the same age as the mammoth, and woolly rhinoceros; and the Neanderthall skull belongs to the same period. It is to be expected, that, at so remote a time, a savage type would be presented. This is more than realized. The contour of the Engis skull agrees with the Australian type, especially in its occipital flattening. The facial bones of both are wanting; and, as these are far more characteristic than the skull, the full relationship cannot be determined. The Neanderthall skull passes by the Australian; and in the heaviness of its ridges, its vertical depression, its sloping occiput, its squamosal sutures, it approaches the ape much more than any other human skull. In internal capacity it rises above the gorilla, but not so far as the latter does above the gibbon, and scarcely more than the largest human brain exceeds the smallest. The largest human skull measured by Morton contained one hundred and fourteen inches; and the smallest, according to Wagner, that of an adult female of ordinary intellect, 55.3 inches. The capacity of the gorilla is 34.5 inches: thus, between the brain of the gorilla and the smallest brain of man, there is only a difference of 10.5 inches, while between the smallest (not idiotic) and largest human brain there is a difference of 58.7 inches.

Whither tend all these facts, if not to place man at the head of the animal world, as the perfected fruit of incomprehensible millenniums of its growth and progress?

CHAPTER III.

ORIGIN OF LANGUAGE.

The Myth of the Tower of Babel. — Is Man the only Being possessing Language? — Growth of Language illustrated in the Romance Tongues. — The Language of Animals. — Intonations of Savage Man. — Ideas of Savages. — Language the Expression of Ideas. — Polysynthesism, its Outgrowths. — Comparison with the Growth of Living Beings. — Fossil Languages a sure Guide in History. — Inevitable Growth of Language. — The Sanskrit. — Rig-Veda. — Difficulty of crossing Languages. — Rapid Changes in the Dialects of Savages. — The great Achievement of Comparative Philology, — the Discovery of an Ancient Tongue to which Sanskrit, Greek, Latin, &c., are mutually related. — Its Method of Research. — What is a just Estimate of the Affinities of Dialects? — Agassiz' Theory of Language opposed. — Conclusions.

PERHAPS no problem has more perplexed philosophers than that of the origin of language. Whence came the wonderful instrument by which thought more subtle and evanescent than lightning could express itself, and, through the secondary means of symbolic characters, array itself in permanent form? The task of furnishing a solution seemed hopeless, when the philosopher looked over the world with its diversity of races, speaking several thousand dialects mutually unintelligible, and considered that these were but a remnant of the tongues which have gone down to oblivion.

In remotest historic time, the question was asked; and the God-fearing Hebrew answered, that, because man thought to evade the dictates of Jehovah by building the Tower of Babel, each went away from that unpropitious labor speaking a different tongue. The myth is beautiful; but we know, that, ages before, there was the same degree of diversity as at present.

The name Babel or Babylon tells us that it was not the tower, but the city, wherein reigned confusion of dialects. Situated on the boundaries of two great branches of speech, it drew within its walls dialects of each. From the word the myth arose, as many have before and since.

Wise men have considered that man could only have possessed language by a miracle. They think that by it he is wholly severed from the animal world. As William von Humboldt expresses it, "Man is man only through the power of speech; but, to possess speech, he must already be man." Thus he stands alone the only speaking being on the earth. If this be true, the acquirement of language is an impossibility: it must have been given him ready formed. An eminent philosopher thinks that it was the work of a conclave of sages. Wonderful, indeed, would have been their mute deliberations: he should tell us how they arrived at their conclusions, having no language wherewith to reason together.

Speculation is scarcely admissible; for, by observation, we can see the rise and steady growth of languages. The six Romance dialects, the English, the German, were all born in historic time. They are recent, and we know that they have developed from pre-existing dialects, as the English from the Latin and Anglo-Saxon, the Romance tongues from a decomposition of Latin; yet no learned body of men ever sat in council to mould their grammatical construction, or give definitions to words of any of them. The mandates of kings have been of small avail in giving tone to popular speech. The change has been gradual. The lisp of childhood, the garrulity of age, the sage and the idiot, have all helped. No one can say when Italian became Italian and not Latin, French became French, Spanish became Spanish. The differentiation was, however, effected; and the seeming difference between the modern dialects is great.

Language is not fashioned by rules of men; it grows by rules established in the constitution of mind: it is not created by reason, but by growth. Primarily, language is but vocalized expression; and, in this sense, all animals have each a tongue peculiar to themselves.

The roar of the lion by its intonation informs all other lions of his feelings and thoughts, whether of hunger, pain, or anger. The wolf's howl of hunger is unlike its call for its companions. The carol of the song-bird, the scream of the eagle, are as expressive as though translated into human speech: we readily understand these simple, unequivocal, vocalizations of passion. They are words of a language unknown to us, except as we understand by intonation and signs. Locke, Monboddo, and others, suppose animals have no language because they do not have abstract ideas. It may be true that they have not; but is language confined to the conveyance of abstract ideas? When the hour-old babe cries, "Ma!" has it abstract ideas? or when it is capable of expressing its wants by an attempted articulation of the name of the object, or in those Oriental negroes wherein language is reduced to its lowest estate, or in the case of the laborers in England whose entire vocabulary is found not to contain three hundred words, how many abstract ideas is this instrument called on to convey? All animals have rudimentary organs of speech, and many have them in great perfection. Why do they not vibrate with thrilling words? Because there is no mind behind the organs, capable of originating thrilling ideas. With the glottis of the gorilla, or even with an artificial one, man could articulate perfectly.

Animals, by the ircharacteristic intonations, express their few and simple thoughts, confined exclusively to their corporeal wants and passions. Between civilized man and the animal there is a tremendous reach of intellect, and perhaps a complete addition of morals. The interval is filled, in a great measure, by savage peoples, and by beings that are now extinct. This difference yields a perfected speech. That intellect and morals express themselves through his organs of speech is as natural and consistent as that the passions should through those of animals. The language of abstract ideas is as natural as the processes of thought by which such ideas are evolved. It is nothing foreign to him, but an outgrowth of mind.

Savage man is born on the globe languageless; but he has thoughts and the organs to express those thoughts, and his first infant cry is the first word of his language. He expresses pain by cries, and laughs when pleased. His language may not be greatly superior to the animals. A hundred words may fully express all his ideas, and those principally names of objects; as animals, trees, places. The relations these bear to each other and to him could be expressed by gestures; for communication in such a state would require more intuition than reason.

Thought necessarily precedes expression; for a word is the symbol of an idea, and could not be created without the idea. As the savage began to have clearer ideas, he would endeavor to express himself with greater clearness: new words would spontaneously arise; and, as they awoke similar ideas in the hearer, when he desired to convey that idea he would use the same word which had conveyed that idea to him; and thus the articulation would come to stand for the idea, leaving a wide margin, however, for gesture. The ideas of savages are not complex, but as simple as those of children. Hence they strive to present them simultaneously by a single effort or word; and from this results agglutination or polysynthesism, a characteristic of ancient and of savage languages. They combine the phrase into a single tightly interlocked word, containing all its appendages and shades of meaning. The language thus formed is composed of stereotyped phrases. The tongue sets forth, with an intonation expressive of the individual's sensation, neither noun, verb, nor adjective, but capable of being either, or all combined. It is a simple expression of feeling, as of joy, pain, or hope.

Such is the elementary condition of all languages, and is preserved in many at present.

As ideas, by the development of mind, became clearer, the necessity of distinguishing the parts of a sentence by which they are expressed becomes evident, and noun and verb are distinguished; words set apart to express action not being used to express the names of things. In Chinese, this stage has not been attained. Traces of the previous condition are met with in English, far away as it is from its original polysynthesism; as the employment of many words as nouns, and also as verbs: as fly, an insect; fly, to move through the air.

Language advances by analysis, by which the parts of a sentence are differentiated from each other, and appropriate offices assigned to each.

When savage man began to aggregate into tribes, each tribe would commence the formation of a language of its own. There would be expressions common to all, based on the anatomical structure of the organs of speech; but, independent of these, each tribe would rapidly acquire new expressions. Those dwelling among mountains, surrounded by the most startling phenomena of Nature, would have quite different sensations from those dwelling on extensive plains. Each would have ideas awakened by surrounding scenes, which the others would not have, and hence words to express those sensations which the others would not have. Man is a creature of circumstances; and the great Humboldt has told in beautiful language how the human heart vibrates to the ever-varying aspects of surrounding Nature.

From this starting-point, the various languages diverge until so widely separated that their origin is lost; and the most expert linguist fails to observe any other relationship, except such as grows out of the similarity of anatomy in all races.

Some tribes have exhausted the forms of expression on the verb, using it as the means of designating the relationship of the sentence; others have used the substantive, to mark by its variations the inter-relation of its dependencies. No language is perfect, and some races express shades of meaning which have remained unrecognized by others. Thus the Sanskrit, so much richer than the Greek in the manner it indicates the relations of a noun to a phrase, of words between themselves, and the nature of the verb, has no mood for a verb distinct from time.

The general mechanism of language is everywhere the same; for that is dependent on the anatomical structure of the brain which originates, and the organs which express thought; and human nature, from the poles to the equator, is very near the same.

When we view this wonderful structure, so harmonious in all its parts; so delicately and logically constituted; expressive of the minutest shade of feeling; capable of conveying the inspirations of Jehovah, or illuminating the darkest province of Nature,—we are lost in amazement, and shrink from referring it to the silent and imperceptible growth of ages.

It appears complete, as the work of one man grasping the wants and feelings of all other men; yet we know by the records of history that it has been built up by the conjoint labors of all men, laboring unknowingly, as bees building in harmony a beautiful and mathematically constructed comb. The philosopher coining a new word to express the scarcely defined shade of meaning he wishes to convey, the playful chance misarticulation of the child, the word of wisdom, the rude utterance of the boor, the polite language of refinement, the slang of the street, even the voice of the wild brute, is incorporated in this structure.

Drawing existence from so many sources, at once seemingly fortuitous and conflicting, how wonderful that each language should be a perfect harmony, and all be related by the deep foundation of their structure! The explanation is very simple. The organs of speech are the same, except the slightest variations, in all races of mankind. They are capable of making but a certain number of distinct articulations or sounds. The imperfect organs of the animal realm cannot make all of these, nor can the rudest races of men; but what they do make are of these, and they can make no others. The song of the bird, and roar or growl of the wild beast, are made with consonants and vowels: all their voices can be expressed by letters. Thus all races have a few simple sounds to build with. There is no language which uses all of these. The choice is probably the result of slight anatomical peculiarities.

These sounds savage man crowds or agglutinizes into one spontaneous expression, as representing an idea or emotion, just as the lion to express anger utters an explosive or prolonged growl, or the wolf a repeated howl. There is simply the expression of feeling heightened by gesture. The phrase is nothing more than a gesture of the tongue. This is what may be considered the rudest state of the language of man. It is sufficient to meet the wants of the savage, as it expresses all his feelings and ideas.

As he advances out of his savagehood, ideas arise independent of objects. The mind not only is capable of receiving ideas of objects, but can unite these simple terms into complex thoughts, and put forth such thoughts as intangible representatives of tangible things. Delicate relations are discovered which cannot be expressed by conglomerated phrases. By analysis the primitive words are disintegrated, and changed to meet the new requirements.

This growth is like that of the development of life, seen in the evolution of the chain of living beings revealed by geology. There is first but one organ to serve all purposes: slowly other organs form to meet various requirements. The assimilation of food is the essential condition of animal life, and hence the first organ is a stomach. The animal is nothing more than a stomach floating in the water; so the cardinal requirement of speech is the expression of thought, and the tongue makes one gesture for that object.

To this simple, floating sac, organs for locomotion; a complicated digestive system, composed of members between whom the labor is divided; circulating nervous systems, the latter receiving impressions of seeing, hearing, feeling, —are added one by one, until it becomes a wonderful being, capable of meeting the most varied requirements.

So from the original phrase-word, which is neither noun, verb, nor other part of speech, but either, or all combined, these parts are developed by a slow process to a complete separation.

If we admit the theory herein advanced, by studying the various tongues from the savage to the civilized, the process by which the advance or growth is made can be readily discerned. For if the most civilized was once in the same condition as the agglutinated tongues of savages, and all are following after the same manner of growth, then the diverse languages of the world become but so many stages through which the highest have passed, and the entire history of growth is revealed.

It is as though language had left fossil remains all along the path of its ascent, and those, too, far less equivocal than those of geology.

It is a living, growing structure, always the perfect photograph of the mind which uses it. It changes from year to year, from century to century; rarely enduring a thousand years. This growth is affected by the aggregation of words from other languages, and the growth of thought coining new words to express itself, or giving new meanings to old words. This process can be observed in every writer or speaker. Often words used in the slang of the vulgar are elevated into polished literature. The developments of science have introduced during the present century many thousand new words, and our lexicons have to be revised every year. Language seeks to become cosmopolitan. As geological knowledge extends, and the facilities for travel and mutual interchange of thought and commodities perfect, each language grasps to itself all others. Each race learns the thoughts of others; and how can the new thought be better expressed than by the words by which it was first conveyed?

Even languages which are held as sacred, and sacrilegious to corrupt, have not been preserved from change and decay. Before the Christian era, Hebrew had ceased to live; and Sanskrit, venerated for ages by the Hindoo as the vehicle of the divine utterance of the Vedas and sacred poems, shared the same fate. It is an easy task to observe the growth of a language. Words retain vestiges of their origin, such as silent letters, not of any use in pronouncing the word, but once employed in the old speech. If we go back any considerable distance, say in English, we shall find that a great many words from which the silent letters have now disappeared then retained them; and by their aid the origin of the words can be determined.

The Sanskrit, the oldest written language, affords the best view of development. It is so intricate and wonderfully complicated, that it astonished the scholars of Europe, who held for a long time that it was an invention of philosophic Brahmins to preserve their knowledge from the common people; but now it is discovered that those common people speak a language which must have grown out of the Sanskrit by ages of decay and corruption. In its first appearance in the Rig-Veda, it has all the inversion, complexity, and agglutinized characteristics of the savage age of spontaneous thought. Then follows the age of analysis, carried to the extent of the decomposition of its grammar. The process then ceases; for the language becomes too unwieldy to be used when brought in collision with the dialect of a conquering race. Here a fact is brought to light of a very interesting nature. When two languages are brought in contact, the more advanced or analytical gains the ascendency. Thus the French tends to supplant German and the Basque-Breton, when the two coalesce on the borders, and in its turn, when spoken by negroes, is simplified in structure to the level of an African tongue.

Languages are difficult to cross from this cause. The barbarians conquered Rome, but lost their language by doing so. The Romance tongues are monuments of the enduring logic of Latin speech. The Anglo-Saxon language only appropriated a few words, and names of places, of the Celto-Britons. The Arab has in vain endeavored to compel his Persian subjects to speak the language of the Koran. They employ Arabic words to such an extent, that whole sentences are spoken in pure Arabic; yet the structure of such sentences remains purely Persian. The modern Greek still uses the idiom of Demosthenes, yet with so changed a vocabulary, that that orator could not understand his modern countrymen. The Turkish, one of the widest-spread languages, so tenaciously retains its Tartarian structure, that the rude Yakat from the frozen regions of Siberia and the polished Turko-Sybarite of luxurious Constantinople, although their ancestors were separated beyond the ken of tradition, are mutually intelligible to each other.

Numerous facts prove that language is of growth, and that its development is due to the expansion of mind. This statement has no reference to the perfection of structure, but to the capability and perfection of conveying thought. Some savage tongues have very perfect structure: this praise must be awarded to all; yet these structures are often complex, and cumbersome in the extreme. It has been a stereotyped speech for centuries with scholars to praise the beauty, sweetness, strength, and power of Greek and other ancient tongues. Allowance must be made for the affection a student has for his particular study, and the fact that the translator always finds many novelties, which, through the interesting method of substituting a word in one language for a corresponding word in another, seems to give that language greater expressive power; but, if the subject be maturely considered, will an Englishman say that he has ideas which his language cannot express with all the beauty, force, and strength it has in his mind? Will a German, a Frenchman, an Italian, acknowledge this of their several tongues? It is said that the word corresponding to *humanity* is vainly sought for in Greek. Can it be supposed, that, if the idea existed, it could have remained unexpressed? Linguists take it for granted that it did not, by the absence of the word. Equally vain would be the search for words expressive of the great modern inventions and scientific discoveries, which may be said to require a distinct language of their own.

Sanskrit, Greek, Latin, even the hieroglyphs of Egypt and the cuneiform inscriptions of Nineveh, can be translated into modern speech; but he who attempted to render a modern book into any of these would stumble at every sentence, and find a host of words for which the ancient speech had no synonymes. Why is this? Is it not simply because the human mind has expanded, and, to express its new thoughts, added to its vocabulary? Greek was perfect for the Greeks, Chaldee for Chaldeans, modern speech for moderns; but how fettered would be our minds were we compelled to express ourselves in any ancient tongue, even were it made our mother's dialect!

The Norwegian colony which settled Iceland in the ninth century remained so stationary, that, at the end of four hundred years, they still spoke nearly pure old Norse, and were unable to converse with the people of their mother-country. The desolate island scenery and isolated social life furnished not even as many ideas as the bleak mountains of Norway and the contact of nationalities.

Germany, during the French wars, as nations always do when thus stimulated, made rapid advances in thought and its expression. A colony sent just previously to the mountains of Pennsylvania, and by the war cut off from the mother-country, were found, only twenty-five years afterwards, to be speaking as Germans had done in the previous century. Their slight contact with the English had fused many English words into their speech, which they used to represent the new objects presented. They had advanced in one direction, Germany in another. Previous to the time of Cicero, the Latin tongue appears to have been in a state of rapid growth or change. Polybius says that the best-informed Romans could with difficulty read the treaties between Carthage and Rome. Horace says he could not understand the Salian Poems; and from Quintilian we learn that the sacred hymns were scarcely understood by the priests.

Latin was once the dialect of a small tribe, — one among many which inhabited Italy. It was more especially the language of Rome. It was the polite tongue. It was not spoken by the plebeians; and, had they gained the mastery previous to the classic age, Latin would have been quite different. It was rapidly changing until Livius, Andronicus, Ennius, Cato, Lucretius, Cicero, and the Scipios, fixed it permanently in literature, very much as Johnson, Shakspeare, and Milton fixed English speech in their writings.

Such a condition is said to necessitate the decay of a language; it rather is a landmark by which the change or advance can be observed. Were it not for literature, we could not observe changes; for literature itself is only a record of change. Missionaries attempted to write the language of the Indians of Central America, and compiled a dictionary containing all the words they could gather. After only ten years, they found their work antiquated and useless; so rapidly had old words sunk into disuse, and new ones arisen.

In the mountain ranges of the Irrawaddy Peninsula, multitudes of tribes speak different dialects; and Capt. Gorden collected in the neighborhood of Maniparu twelve dialects, some of which were not spoken by more than forty families; and Brown says that tribes who have removed to neighboring valleys, after two or three generations, were unintelligible to those they left in their native valley. The Ostiac has degenerated into so many dialects, that people dwelling not twenty miles apart are unintelligible to each other. It seems, according to Castrén, that the barbarous tongues of the Buriates and Tungusic idioms around Njertschinsk, Siberia, are rapidly growing, and have surpassed the literary mongolian; having added terminations expressive of the persons of verbs, which the latter has not.

Travellers never fail to experience profound surprise at the diversity of dialects in Africa. Moffat describes how this diversity occurs. In the isolated villages of the desert, the children are left in the care of the aged while the parents set off on long journeys, lasting for weeks or months. "The infant progeny, some of which are beginning to lisp, while others can just master a whole sentence, and those still further advanced, romping and playing together, the children of Nature, through their livelong day, become habituated to a language of their own. . . . Thus from this infant Babel proceeds a dialect of a host of mongrel words and phrases joined together without rule; and, in the course of one generation, the entire character of the language is changed." In the absence of any method by which words are recorded, it will be readily seen, that, when these children mature, their language will be retained, while the death of their parents will destroy the link which unites them to the past.

The countless Indian tribes, from the Esquimaux of the Arctic Ocean to the Patagonian of Terre del Fuego, speak dialects unintelligible to each other. Here, as in Africa, language is in a state of constant flux, and words are evanescent symbols, enduring scarcely a single generation.

Great as are the fluctuations in the vocabulary of languages, their grammatical structure is far more permanent; and their relationship is established from this fact in a more permanent manner than possible by the mere correspondence of words.

Comparative philology is recent, scarcely dating back to the beginning of the present century; but it has been cultivated with great assiduity, engaging the strongest intellects, and has made startling revelations in the new field it has opened.

Its greatest achievement is the discovery of an ancient central language from which the old historic tongues were derived, and placing its site in Central Asia. As the Italian, Spanish, Portuguese, French, Wallachian, and Rhætian dialects demonstrate that they were derived from a more ancient and common tongue, the Latin; so Latin, Greek, Sanskrit, Zeud, Lithuranian, Sclavonic, Gothic, and Armenian, demonstrate, by their similarity of structure, their common derivation from an ancient tongue. It would not be difficult, were history destroyed, to prove that the Romance languages were derived from a common source, nor more difficult to prove that the eight mentioned ancient tongues must have been derived from one common ancient stock.

Comparative philology has arrived at this grand result by first ascertaining the laws which languages follow in their growth; for, fortuitous as the coining of words may appear, their birth and death are governed by inexorable law. By ascertaining the method by which words change, by phonetic substitution, it is able to trace words back to their roots which would not otherwise have been thus referred. To illustrate what is meant by roots, and to show the irresistible proofs they furnish of the common origin of tongues, we will take a word, and, after extracting its root, show how it unites distant languages. *Respectable* is a word derived from the Latin *respectabilis*. The latter word is composed by affixing *bilis* to the verb *respectare;* separate the prefix *re*, and *spectare*, a participle from *specere*, to see, remains. This latter is compounded of the unchangeable *spec*, and changeable *ere*. The word can be reduced no farther; and hence spec is the root of respectable, or rather the original first coined word from which all words containing it sprang, such as respect, respec-tive-ly, respite, de-spise, circumspect, suspicion, and a host of others, all having their synonymes in the other branches of Assyrian speech. *Spec*, in Sanskrit, is spás; in old high German, *spëka;* in Greek, *skep*. If a root is found in one Aryan tongue, it will be found in the others, having nearly the same meaning, although the words which grow out of it may be very different, and have changed their meaning.

The number of roots is small compared with the number of words. Sanskrit has but 1,706, according to the older grammars; and recent students have reduced the number to 500 by tracing words back to more primitive elements. Hebrew contains 500; Chinese, 450, multiplied by accents and intonations to 1,263, producing a dictionary of 50,000 words.

With five hundred roots like *spás*, *spec*, a language like the English, containing one hundred thousand words, is readily composed. How few of these words are used! There are laborers in England who are said not to use over three hundred words; and a well-educated person seldom uses more than four thousand: eloquent speakers, not more than ten thousand; Shakspeare, the most original of English writers, fifteen thousand; Milton, not more than eight thousand; the Old Testament, five thousand six hundred and forty-two. The writers of the hieroglyphics, the sages of Egypt, wrote all their thoughts with two thousand and thirty words, according to the most recent research.

The savage Indian of America, or the more barbarous negro of Africa, cannot have a more extended vocabulary than the English laborer; and consequently the substitution of new for old terms more quickly affects the character of their speech.

Having shown the manner in which the roots, the fundamental elements of language, are determined, the proof they afford will be appreciated. These are briefly, —

1. There existed a parent race in Central Asia. 2. That the Latin, Greek, Sanskrit, Zend, Lithuranian, Sclavonic, Gothic, and Armenian were branches sent off from this parent stock. 3. That this separation occurred while these peoples were in a semi-savage state.

All these propositions are proved by tracing out the words held in common by these eight branches. Not only their common origin, but the social advancement they each had attained before they separated from that parent stem, can be determined. Thus the names for ox, sheep, horse, goose, and dog, are the same in all, as are those for carts, yokes, and fixed habitations; showing that, before their separation, all these animals had been domesticated, these implements been constructed, and the wandering savage began to learn the use of a fixed dwelling. The sameness of the words for numbers, and the lunar divisions of the year, show that they divided the year by the mutations of the moon, and counted to more than one hundred by the decimal system, and worshipped according to the system revealed in the Rig-Vedas.

The seat of the parent dialect is traced towards the East, or to Central Asia, by the constant approach the languages met with in that direction make towards what may be considered a common stock, or towards the Sanskrit, its eldest offspring, and the departure made from it towards the west, where, in the extreme continental limits, the Celtic is so remote, that for a long time it was considered as belonging to another and distinct group.

The elements of the European languages are found in the Sanskrit, like remnants of one mother-tongue. They are more logical, more analytic, but not, as philologists are wont to say of modern dialects, impoverished. To suppose a language three thousand years old, expressing the ideas of that time, superior to a language embodying the thoughts, inventions, and magnificent discoveries of the present is too absurd to need refutation.

There has been a tendency, and it is of German

origin, belonging to German thought and erudition, to elevate language above anatomy in the classification of the races of men; in other words, to place more dependence on the relationship of the dialects of the races, than agreement of form, color, or structure. This may appear strange; but it is found true, that, after a people have attained sufficient advancement to acquire what may comparatively be called a permanent speech, the essential elements of that speech are retained more tenaciously than the physical characteristics of the race.

Words are the habiliments of the soul, and partake of its own indestructible qualities. The deeper the research is carried, the more certain it appears that structure of language is more permanent than race. Who for instance would classify the swart Hindoo and the florid German together? yet language places them near, very near, to each other; and, having thus obtained the indication, or lead, and based himself on a true classification, the scholar finds ethnological reasons to support his linguistic conclusions.

On the other hand, eminent men have wholly ignored the truthfulness of language in classification. Agassiz has given his name to this issue. He compares the brumming of the bears of Thibet, East Indies, Nepaul, Syria, Europe, Siberia, the Rocky Mountains, and the Andes, which, though of different species, utter the same sound; the miawing of the cats of Europe, Asia, Africa, and America; the gackling of gallinaceous birds, the song of the thrushes; and concludes, "Let any philologist study these facts, and learn at the same time how independent these animals are from the other, which utter such closely allied systems of intonations, and, if he be not altogether blind to the significance of the analogies of Nature, he must begin himself to question the reliability of philological evidence as proving genetic origin."

This conclusion merits repetition only from its source. It shows a want of appreciation of the principles which govern linguists. The sounds made by these orders of animals may be, and perhaps are, inherited from a primitive common ancestor, and point to such an origin; but, be that as it may, the words which possibly agree by reason of anatomical similarity are discarded, and such only are used in comparison as are unmistakably free from such criticism. What is more, it is on grammatical structure the main reliance is placed; for that is more enduring than the words it controls.

That the eight great branches should, if isolated, each invent the decimal system, and call the numbers by similar names, would be beyond possibility. That they should call any number by the same name would be impossible; but that they should call a hundred alike, and not only that, but give similar names to their domestic animals, their dwellings and occupations, is entirely beyond belief.

This proof, drawn from the most permanent part of language, is strengthened by the deeper structure of these tongues. The idiom employed by the peasant of Germany is repeated by the sanctified Brahmin in his devotions before the altar of Brahma. Tenaciously as the grammar is retained, it breaks before we reach the lowest race, and in this, and in this alone, fails to be all that is required of a method of classification. Aided by history, in all the nationalities of the world it speaks unmistakably except of the Oriental negro and some fragments of tribes whom it fails to connect with the great stem which supports the other races.

These lowest peoples were cast off before the fixation of speech. We have seen how, among a certain grade of savages, language is in a constant flux; and a few years or a single year change its nature. Not until it attains to a degree of permanence, the result of superior advancement, can we look for the preservation of its distinctive marks.

This stage was not attained, as the present classification indicates, until after the separation of the two great branches,— the TURANIAN and ARYAN.

CHAPTER IV.

ORGANIC AND CLIMATIC CHANGES.

Geographical Dispersion of Organic Beings in Relation to Man. — The Great Zoölogical Provinces first distinctly marked immediately antecedent to the Introduction of Man. — Cause of. — Climate of the Earth during the Tertiary. — Disappearance of Climatic Distinctions in the Secondary Strata. — Zoölogical Provinces of the Earth, — the Arctic Realm, the Asiatic, the European, the African, the Australian, the Indian, the Polynesian. — Realms, how defined, how produced. — The Principles applicable to the Dispersion of Animals also applicable to the Dispersion of the Races of Men.

The geographical distribution of organic forms, the subdivisions of the zoölogical provinces wherein peculiar types flourish to the exclusion of others, is first noticeable in the age immediately antecedent to the introduction of man; and it is a remarkable fact, that the zoölogical provinces of the earth immediately preceding the drift correspond with those of the present. The kangaroo, *dinornis*, &c., are not found in the Europeo-Asiatic province, but in the Australian; the rhinoceros, hyena, lion, &c., belong to the African; while the elephant, mammoth, rhinoceros, bear, hyena, hare, &c., roamed the European, the mastodon, megatherium, megalonyx, glyptodon, mylodon, toxodon, macrauchema, and other extinct beings, inhabited the American continent; the former pointing to species existing at present on the continent, the latter to forms more changed, but of the same type; as the llama, cava, capabara, sloth, and armadillo. The monkey race indicates the same fact. Their fossils found in Brazilian caverns belong to the platyrrhine family, now peculiar to South America.

Holding firmly to the principle that organic forms in their introduction and maintenance are governed by law, and that they are progressive in development, we must search for the cause or causes of geographical distribution in the laws which regulate the climate of the globe. If a uniform climate prevailed over the whole earth, one fauna and one flora only could exist. In proportion as climate changes shall we meet with changes in the organic beings subjected to its influence.

Until the tertiary age, there was a nearly uniform climate. During the coal period, the lepidodendron, sigillaria, and palm flourished from the arctic to the antarctic circle; and the fossil remains of saurian, denizens of warm seas, are scattered over the world, regardless of present climatic dictinctions.

Until that age, paleontology records only extinct species, and generally extinct *generæ*. Its records of each age are fragments of the preceding, as existing species strike their roots into the generæ of the fossil world. Each age presents new species; but they are closely related to the age immediately past.

This differentiation of climate undoubtedly began in the earliest ages, but not until the tertiary had it become sufficient to produce marked results. As mountain chains gave shape to continental masses, as existing oceans, currents, islands, and the elevation of the land, became like the present, and the radiation of the earth's central heat allowed the influence of the sun to be locally felt, the climate of different portions of the earth began to assume their present character; and, with this change in climate, living beings became subject to local influences, and hence localized.

At the closing age of the tertiary, the PLEISTOCENE, or DRIFT, three-fourths of the fossil shells are of existing *species,* and most of the principal generæ of mammals correspond to those of the same zoölogical provinces.

In the age immediately preceding, the PLIOCENE, one-third the species of mollusks, and nearly all the mammalia, are extinct.

In the next lower and earlier age, about two-thirds of the shells are extinct; and those that still exist must be looked for, not in adjoining seas, but in latitudes to the south, indicating a differentiation of climate: in other words, the *temperate zone* was being established on the borders of the far-reaching but then contracting torrid. All the fossil mammals of that age are extinct.

Here we may notice that the higher orders of all classes of animate existence are less able to withstand the vicissitudes of conditions than the lower. They are products of favored circumstances, and modelled to meet certain requirements, and yield obedience more slowly to the new. It is not the gigantic and aberrant beings, as the margatherium, mylodon, and mammoth, the megalasaums, masosaurus, and iguanodon, which survive, but shell-fish and zoöphytes, coming up from the dark night of the silures to dwell in the sunshine of the present seas, scarcely modified in generic distinctions. Such instances are rare; but they serve to show the tenacity with which the hereditary powers of life preserve their identity against adverse conditions, and how slowly the forces of change operate. The little TERRABRATULA has withstood conditions which have swept the fleets of huge saurians from the ocean, levelled the coal forests of the coal measures, and buried in ruins the herds of mammoths and mastodons which roamed from the Yellow Sea, across both continents, to the Pacific Ocean.

In the EOCENE, the oldest portion of the tertiary, reposing directly above the secondary rocks, the relation between the present and ancient zoölogical provinces disappears. With few exceptions, all its shells are extinct; and those still living are found in torrid latitudes. All its mammifers belong to extinct species, and the greater part to extinct GENERÆ, indicating changes so great as to obliterate radical characteristics. The fossil plants of its upper portion indicate a climate like that of Southern Europe and the Mediterranean, while those in its lowest show a tropical climate.

As we pass down into the secondary strata, all climatic distinctions disappear. It is, then, of the deep sea, or shallow river or ocean, lake or estuary, that we observe these influences, and not of the more powerful force of temperature which now renders the poles masses of uninhabitable ice, the equator a burning zone, and the intermediate spaces temperate regions.

Having indicated the differentiation of climate, we are prepared to view with comprehending glance the distinguishing features of the zoölogical provinces into which this differentiation divides the surface of the earth.

The broad field covered by the term "climate" includes not only the thermal and meteorological conditions of a country, but all external circumstances brought to bear on living beings. It includes, even in meteorological sense, the configuration and elevation of the land; as it is evident that climate is intimately related to physical geography, or the elevation and depression of continents and islands, mountains and valleys, currents in air and ocean, and all the diversified aspects assumed by the physical world.

Beginning with an all-enveloping ocean studded with islands, and a high uniform temperature arising from the internal heat of the earth, as mountains were pushed upwards, and continents showed their broad backs above the sea, arresting the flow of currents in the sea and atmosphere; as the lands assumed their present aspect, the provinces of life were defined more and more clearly, until, by loss of internal heat, the thermal conditions depended entirely on the sun's rays: thus the globe was divided into unchanging zones of temperature, and the universal province became subdivided, as at present, at nearly the same time with the appearance of existing species of animals and of man.

Of these provinces, we shall first consider the Arctic Realm. This extends from the North Pole, irregularly beyond the Arctic Circle, to the northern limits of forests. It is characterized by the uniformity with which its animals and plants are distributed. It is remarkable that plants become dwarfed, stunted, and wholly disappear, while animal life flourishes in vigor, and pushes its most gigantic forms far beyond into the Frozen Sea. Some graminiferous plants, mosses and lichens, serve as a scanty pasture to the ruminants and rodents. Flowering plants are of few species; but some of them make up in number of individuals the deficiency of kinds, often when in bloom resembling drifts of snow. A month is sufficient for them to mature their seeds, which feed a few small birds. The gull, and other sea-side feeders, prey on the immense swarms of fish, or marine plants and infusoria. Countless flocks of geese, ducks, petrels, penguins, cormorants, and gulls larger than eagles, hover over the coast and islands. The mammals are the white bear, musk-ox, reindeer, white fox, polar hare, lemming, walrus, cachalot, seal, norwal, and whale. Fishes are numerous, and the lower order of worms, mollusks, echinoderms, and medusæ, are well represented; but not a single reptile dwells in this zone. Its flora is devoid of all plants used as food by civilized man; and its dwarfed races of men who dwell on the borders of the frozen ocean are compelled to live on an almost exclusive flesh diet, relieved only by a miserable lichen, the tripe-de-roche. They have only two domestic animals: in the east, the reindeer; in the west, the dog. This realm is distinguished by the sharpness of its outline. South of it, lies first the AMERICAN REALM, characterized by the wide diffusion of its species, a fact referable to the mountain-chain extending from the Arctic Circle to Patagonia, furnishing a means of transit. Thus we find many ancient plants and animals common to both North and South America.

Tropical America does not possess the luxuriance of species of Africa. Its largest pachyderms are insignificant, and its ruminants small in comparison. The tapir and peccary represent the former; the llama and alpaca, the latter. Species rivalling the elephant of Africa flourished at a recent period, as the mastodon, megatherium, &c.; but they are extinct, with the horse it once possessed. It approaches Australia in possessing marsupials; but its ostriches are different generically from those of that continent, and its monkeys are not generically represented in Africa.

The next realm, bordering the Arctic, and almost joining the American, is the Asiatic, remarkable for being the original home of the progenitors of the domestic horse, ox, sheep, and goat. It possesses the musk-deer, the bear, argali, yak, the bactrian camel, the wild horse and ass, and numberless other forms. It extends from the Arctic Circle to the Himalaya, from the Pacific to the borders of Europe, and may be considered as one vast and greatly elevated table-land. Its exposure to the unmitigated Arctic blasts depresses its temperature. At a recent geological date, probably since the advent of man, the elephant and rhinoceros roamed over the now inhospitable steppes of Siberia to the mouth of the Lena on the Frozen Ocean.

The European Realm extends from the Arctic Circle to the deserts of Sahara, from the western boundaries of Asia to the Atlantic. Its representative animals are the bear, stag, antelope, goat, aurochs, and wolf.

The African Realm, embracing the whole of the African continent, except a narrow border along the Mediterranean, possesses one of the highest types of the animal kingdom, as well as the largest,—the chimpanzee (*troglodytes niger*), the elephant, rhinoceros, hippopotamus, giraffe, lion, tiger, leopard, and innumerable antelopes and deer, and its representative species.

The Australian Realm embraces all that continent, and is entirely unique: it is exclusively represented by marsupials, as the opossum and kangaroo.

The Indian Realm embraces all Asia south of the Himalaya, and the many islands lying between Australia and Hindostan. Its animals are the elephant, rhinoceros, tapir, stag, and the highest of animals, the pithecus satyrus, or orang outang.

The Polynesian Realm embraces the islands scattered throughout the Pacific Ocean, and is characterized more by its races of men than animals. It is entirely fragmentary, and its fragments are set in a wide ocean, often hundreds of miles apart.

The Arctic Realm is limited on its southern border by the increasing temperature. Its fauna, being adapted to withstand a vigorous temperature, are disqualified for sustaining heat: even when the sun for a few weeks melts the ice and snow from the southern faces of the hills, and brown lichens start in the warmest nooks, oppressed by the heat, its inhabitants crowd towards the pole. The whale loves the coldest bays of icebergs, and to bathe in water far below freezing. The sea of the tropics would be to it an impassable sea of fire. Surrounded by a coat of blubber a foot or more in thickness, which, at the same time, retains and supplies heat, it seems constantly overstocked with caloric, in a high fever which nothing but ice can satisfy. The seal and the walrus are protected in like manner, and the bear and musk-ox are clad in thickest fur.

The ANTARCTIC REALM is scarcely known: as it has no land except what is buried beneath perpetual ice, its fauna is exclusively of the sea. The whale, seal, and penguin are its characteristic forms; but these are of different species from those of the Arctic. The whale cannot cross the tropic, and hence its diffusion must have occurred previous to the present differentiation of climate. The American Realm is, except beyond the Arctic Circle, cut off by vast oceanic expanses from all others. The European Realm is isolated on the west by an ocean, on the east by seas and mountains, on the south by the Saharian wastes. The African and Australian are isolated by a surrounding ocean. The Asiatic Realm has an ocean north and east, and the almost impassable Himalaya on the south. Having thus briefly surveyed the realms into which the earth is divided by barriers now existing, we are enabled to understand how this differentiation has been attained. If we glance at a geological map, we shall see that the land during the earlier tertiary did not have its present form.

The salient features existed; mountain ridges showed their sharp outlines from the sea, anticipating the future form of the continents: but, even so late, the character of the land was essentially insular. Projecting masses, since submerged, brought the Old and New Worlds into close relationship. This, in connection with a uniform temperature, favored the wide distribution of species.

With these realms, as yet faintly defined, but rapidly developing their peculiarities, see how it would be with the diversified species submitted to their agency. Admitting that living beings are resultants of the conditions which originate and surround them, they of course assume forms adapted to those conditions. In the strife for existence, those individuals, species, or generæ, which cannot conform, inevitably perish. Wide seas, swift currents, and mountain barriers, would separate the realms of life. These were introduced slowly. There was opportunity for dissemination and interblending. Then, when thoroughly isolated, each species followed the direction imparted by its parentage, modified by the new circumstances. Many perish; for they are unyielding, or incapable of mastering more vigorous antagonists. Others prosper, and crowd out less plastic forms. But here I take all this for granted, and apply it to the geographical distribution of species in their relation to that of mankind.

The bear of the Rocky Mountains, the black bear of America, the brown bear of Europe and Asia, the white bear of the Arctic, are so intimately related, that the most superficial observer at once pronounces them all bears; yet they differ much more in external appearance than anatomical structure. It is difficult for the anatomist to distinguish between their skeletons.

The puma, and fossil lion of America, the tiger, lion, and leopard of Africa, all present the same uniformity. Cuvier confessed himself unable to distinguish a skull of a lion from that of a tiger. The fossil elephant of America and the existing Asiatic species are very similar. The wolf of America and that of Europe cannot be distinguished by their skulls. This similarity extends to all generæ of animals. It shows a bond of union which cannot be satisfactorily accounted for otherwise than by referring families so related to a common parentage. If we suppose the American fauna to have originated on American soil, and the European on European, it would be inexplicable how the bear, wolf, horse (fossil), the elephant (fossil), lion (fossil), and innumerable other types, should, in countries so remote, surrounded by such diverse conditions, arrive at identical developments. The occurrence of one instance would be remarkable, that of hundreds incomprehensible. That America and Europe each possess a bear, the structures of which cannot be distinguished, together with numberless other instances of conformity, as in deer, wolves, foxes, &c., points to an anterior time when both held a fauna in common. Diversity of conditions has produced specific changes, which are scarcely more than change of color.

It is evident that any theory which accounts for the dispersion of the family of bears or wolves or deer in a partial measure is applicable to the diffusion of the races of men. It appears that the dispersion, or rather specific change, of the latter began about the same time with the former, and must, consequently, have been governed by the same causes.

When we cast every vestige of miracle from science, the justness of this conclusion will be apparent.

CHAPTER V.

THE UNITY OF MANKIND.

Definition of *Species*. — Points of Agreement of all the Races of Men. — Longevity. — Contagious Diseases. — Color of Skin. — Color of Eyes and Hair. — Texture of Hair. — Similar Variations observed in Animals. — Albinos. — Anatomical Comparison of the Races. — Measurements and Comparison of Skulls of. — Hybridity. — Egyptian Records. — CONCLUSIONS.

THAT what are called the RACES or TYPES of mankind belonged to one species is supposed to be proved by their conforming to the tests employed to define species. Species has been defined as "a primordial organic form," and the definition widely received; but it is a problem to solve what is meant by the word "*primordial*." According to the most recent views of naturalists, there are no "primordial" forms. The learned Pritchard defines species: "It includes only the following conditions; namely, separate origin and distinction of race, evinced by the constant transmission of some characteristic peculiarity of organization. Permanent varieties are those, which, having once taken place, continue to be propagated in the breed in perpetuity. The fact of their origination *must be known* by observation or inference; since, the proof of this fact being defective, it is more philosophical to consider characters which are perpetual as specific or original."

From this definition of species, it will be seen that much difficulty invests the subject. Varieties which originated beyond the reach of history must be considered as species; while an equal amount of variation, when known to have occurred, creates, not species, but varieties.

But there are certain tests which can be applied that obviates the necessity of historic data. It has been found that the individuals of a species of animals agree in longevity, in the regularity of periodic changes in their organism, in the diseases (especially contagious) to which they are liable; and that species remotely allied will not produce offspring, and, when nearly allied, their offspring are sterile.

As will be shown, all races of men conform to the requirements of these tests, and must be classed as *permanent varieties.* But, as we shall have occasion to show hereafter, the distinctions are as great as those between the members of the bear, the dog, or the cat families, which most naturalists consider quite sufficient to establish specific relations. As was intimated in a previous chapter, the intimate relation of the members of these families indicates a common origin equally as much as the same relation existing between the races of men. To the latter we for the present will confine our attention.

Taking into consideration the great variation in the conditions of life of the various nationalities of the world, some frozen in and confined to their ice huts half the year, while others are scorched beneath the tropics, and others still enjoy every intermediate grade of climate from lofty and cold mountain-sides to warm valleys, from arid deserts to grassy steppes, it is notable that all attain an almost equal longevity. Some writers have supposed that the difference in length of life was a distinctive race-mark; but more careful investigation shows, that, among all races, individuals occasionally attain a great age, and that an octogenarian is almost equally rare among all.

Savage nations are shorter lived than civilized, — a necessary consequence of their mode of life, and not referable to any distinction of race. The European in the middle ages was quite as short-lived. Dr. Winterbottom speaks of the inhabitants of Guinea as short-lived, and becoming really old at forty-five; but the descendants of these short-lived, because improvident and savage negroes, in the Southern States, where they enjoy many of the comforts of civilization, are among the longest-lived people in the world. Negroes in the West Indies frequently attain the age of one hundred, and sometimes one hundred and twenty.

The Indians have been said to be short-lived, and to mature and decay early; but they often reach the age of ninety and one hundred years. The Laplanders, situated in the extreme north of Europe, are subjected to a rigorous climate, and it is certain that they early attain maturity: they often reach eighty, ninety, and one hundred years. In cold climates and in warm, the age of puberty is attained earlier than in temperate regions, heat and cold producing the same effect. The same may be said of cities over the country, as the more stimulating diet, and associations of the former, have a strong influence. But this period differs but a few years at most, and there is as much variation in any one race as there is between those the most remote.

Neither longevity, nor the period of puberty, furnishes any marks of distinction of race.

If we except malarious influences, to which the African seems acclimated, the different races of men are equally effected by contagious diseases. There are some of these diseases that are communicated by all warm-blooded animals to each other, as hydrophobia; but most such diseases are chiefly confined to the species with which they originate. The most contagious disease among sheep will not extend to oxen or swine; nor will such as the pneumonia extend to horses, although fatal to oxen. Plants show the same quality, — diseases like the yellows in peaches, or black-knot in plums, extending only to those species.

Each species has its own peculiar diseases, which are readily transmitted to the members of the species, but wholly incommunicable to members of other species.

In this manner, all the races of man are shown to belong to one family; for the contagious diseases which affect them do not reach downward, even to the apes, and have a wide margin from all other animals, while they are all similarly affected by the same epidemic or contagion, although some races not as severely as others. Thus the small-pox has spread from the Arctic Ocean to the circumference of Africa, and is equally fatal to the African and the Kamskatdale, all races having been alike scourged.

The Asiatic cholera, the rubeolas, the plague, and syphilis, spare no race.

Pritchard informs us that the yaws is not peculiar to Africans, but is communicable to Europeans.

The elephantiasis prevails among the inhabitants of particular countries, and is produced by peculiarity of food and climate; but, when the system is thus prepared, it is no respecter of race. It is common with the negroes of Guinea, spread into Java in 1661, and attacks Mongolians and Tartars.

When Europeans visit tropical Africa, they usually have fevers produced by malaria, from which the negro population have been erroneously thought to be exempt. The negro has the fevers remittent and intermittent but rarely and lightly; but the negroes who emigrated from the Northern United States to Sierra Leone suffered much more from these fevers. The Indian, when carried to a tropical climate, suffers from the same malarious diseases as the whites. The Aztecs are said to have suffered from what is supposed to have been the yellow fever.

These diseases affect all races, black, yellow, red, and white, but some more than others. The negro cannot withstand diseases which depress vitality, like the plague, cholera, small-pox, or typhoid, or any morbific poison, except malaria. They are predisposed to consumption when living in a cold climate, and are more subject than the whites to inflammatory diseases, and will not bear depletion.

The Semite is peculiarly liable to ophthalmia and cutaneous diseases, such as leprosy.

Individual instances occur of Europeans being quite

as exempt from fevers, dysentery, and other effects of tropical malaria, as the native Africans; and consumption is as certainly fatal to the white as to the black.

The American Indian will endure a severity of cold almost incredible; but arctic explorers have shown that whites could endure a winter in the arctic zone quite as well.

That the African is a child of the tropics, and the white of the temperate zone, is evident; but they are not removed sufficiently by this fact to subject them to different diseases.

It may be stated as a general rule, without exception, that any disease contagious among whites will be so among blacks or red Indians. As such diseases go no further than man, and as among animals each disease is confined to a species, how avoid concluding that all the races of men belong to a common family?

The color of the skin is so different, varying from an almost pure white through yellow and red to jetty black, that it has been used as an unequivocal race-mark; but there are so many intermediate gradations between these, that, by the best naturalists, they are considered of little value. The color of the skin depends on the pigment excreted from the blood, and interposed between the cutis and cuticle. This seems to be excreted from the surface of the cutis, and, like the cuticle, is extravascular. It is as thick as the cuticle in the negro, and, by nice manipulation, can be detached as a separate membrane. It was an old idea that the condition of the liver affected the color of the skin, and this idea has been revived by the eminent and acute Draper. The torpor of the liver, induced by a hot climate, throws the burden of excreting carbon on the skin, and hence the excreted deposit beneath the cuticle. There may be truth in this; but there are other differences of race accompanying change of color which remain unaccounted for.

According to dissections made by Sœmmerring and Hunter, the texture of this intermediate lamella between the cutis and cuticle exists in the fairest of Europeans; but the pigment is not deposited, and hence the color depends on the transparency of the skin revealing the blood in the capillaries beneath. From white to black, every conceivable shade is produced by the amount of coloring-matter deposited in this lamella or rete-mucosum.

From the jetty African, we pass, by insensible degrees, to the brunette of Southern Europe. Exposure to the sun of dark-haired but fair-skinned Spaniards makes them as brown as Arabs or Berbers. The women of swarthy races, when excluded from the sun, are much whiter than the men. The stimulus of light and heat is required to produce the secretion. The same process takes place in whites exposed to the weather, as sailors and voyagers, but to a limited extent; and, as soon as the exposure ceases, the secretion is arrested, and the natural color returns.

The color of the eyes and hair corresponds usually to the color of the skin. The choroid or iris of the eye is colored by a pigment secreted from the surface of the choroid, and passes through the various shades of blue, gray, brown, and black. Light or blue eyes usually accompany a fair, and dark eyes a dark complexion. This is not as unvarying as the color of the hair. The florid complexion is accompanied by flaxen or red hair; and the color of skin accompanying black hair is never so light as that associated with flaxen hair. The deposition of coloring-matter in the hair occurs by a similar and related process to that which colors the skin. The hairs grow from bulbs situated just beneath the cuticle. The hairs are enveloped in a sheath which passes through the skin to the surface. Each hair is formed by an external, transparent, horny sheath, similar in substance to the nails, and an internal pith in which the color of the hair resides. This pith must possess a limited vascular motion, as it undergoes rapid changes of color in disease, or strong mental excitement; a few days or hours sometimes serving to change the color of the hair to snowy white. Unless there was circulation in the hair, this could not occur, nor could the color change with age.

The structure of hair is the same in all races of men and in animals; nor does the structure of wool differ essentially from that of hair; both grow from similar bulbs. Wool issues from smaller bulbs, and is usually waved, so as to possess the property of matting. What has been styled "wool" of Africans is true hair, but is wavy. It is not always short, but in certain papua tribes grows so long as to be brushed out into a periwig three feet across. Some negro tribes have curled hair, not crisp.

Europeans have curled hair; and, if we pass in a direct line from Egypt to the Cape of Good Hope, we shall find every variety of hair from the straight to the most crisp.

The same variations are seen in animals. Varieties

of swine are white, red, and black, and covered with stout bristles, and with crisped hair, or wool. Some varieties of sheep and goats are covered with coarse hair, others with wool. When sheep of the finest grade of wool are transferred to a warmer climate, in a few generations they become covered with coarse hair. The common goat is covered with rough hair; but the Angora goat is covered with long silky hairs of great length and snowy whiteness, and the Cashmere goat produces a fibre of extreme fineness, from which the Cashmere shawls are made.

Some varieties of dog are covered by a thick wool.

All travellers have observed that the color of the individuals of barbarous tribes is not uniform. This is easily explained by calling such tribes "mixed," but not satisfactorily. The fact is too universal to allow of such interpretations. It is rather because varieties arise as it were spontaneously, as they are seen to do among animals.

One of the widest departures is made by albinos, or "white negroes." Their blanched color may result from disease, but, if so, is congenital, and capable of hereditary transmission. There have been many cases of albinos among the slaves in the Southern States, and they are of frequent occurrence in Africa. Whatever the cause in man, the same affects animals. In the albino negro, the hair is white, and the eyes pink. There is a complete absence of the pigment which gives the black color to the negro.

Domestic species of animals often give birth sporadically to albinos. The farmer is often surprised to see cats, dogs, rabbits, sheep, hogs, goats, and horses, give birth to white offspring, while they are of an opposite color. There is scarcely a species of wild animal or bird, but it has been recorded that snowy-white individuals have been seen, as the monkey, squirrel, marten, buffalo, camel, elephant, rhinoceros, deer, badger, beaver, crows, blackbirds, canaries, fowls, and so on to the end.

Among domestic species, varieties often as suddenly spring up of a jetty black; and instances occur of intermediate colors. Sheep are white, red, and black; and cats and dogs sport in an endless variety of color, as do horses and cattle.

With animals as with man, the skin and hair are strictly correlated or dependent, the latter being always of the color of the former; and, when spotted, the skin from which the white, red, or black hairs grow, is of corresponding color.

In structure there exist no considerable variations. The foramen magnum in Africans is placed more forward of the spinal column than in Europeans, in this respect approaching the apes. The ribs are heavier and more arched; the pelvic bones narrower and thinner; the arms are longer, as are the fingers and toes; the bones of the leg are bent outward, so that the knees stand farther apart; the calves of the leg are thin and high, the feet are flat and broad, the hands thin, and fingers flexible. All these departures of the African from the European are made toward the anthropoid apes; but they are not any greater than is made by individual Europeans. It is easy to find individuals of the latter with arms as long as the African, with as thin hands, as long and flexible fingers, with as small and high calves to his legs, as flat feet. On the other hand, no more difficulty is experienced in finding negroes with as short arms as Europeans.

These comparisons might be extended to all races with similar results. None of these superficial characters are sufficiently permanent or defined to be valuable as positive race-marks. All the races flow together at their borders; and it is at the centre, and not at the margins, of their broad streams, that distinctions are discernible.

I will present another point of agreement of races which lies at the foundation of intellectual and moral development. The skull, as it contains the organ of mind, the brain, and by its form indicates that of the enclosed organ, and by its capacity the size of that organ, is of vital consideration. On the skull and teeth the comparative anatomist bases distinctions of species, and he finds no marks as permanent or reliable. Between the teeth of the races of men there is no essential difference. Those of Egyptian mummies are broader than those of Europeans, but no broader than may be readily found among the latter. Instances of double front teeth, and corresponding large molars, are by no means rare. Even this, the most remarkable distinction, is far from being sufficient to establish a specific distinction. From measurements made of the celebrated and extensive Mortonian collection of skulls, the following results have been obtained: —

Of 38 skulls of the Teutonic Family, the internal capacity of the largest was 114 inches; of the smallest 65. Of 9 skulls of the Tchudic family, of the largest was 112.5; of the smallest, 81.5. Of 6 Keltic, of the largest, 97; of the smallest, 78. Of 3 Arabic skulls, of the largest, 98; of the smallest, 84. Of 18 Fellahs, of the largest, 96; of the smallest, 66. Of 10 Chinese skulls, of the largest, 98; of the smallest, 70. Of 20 Malay skulls, of the largest, 97; of the smallest, 68. Of 177 skulls of the ancient Peruvians and Mexicans, the largest, 101; the smallest, 58. Of 164 skulls of American Indians, of the largest, 104; the smallest, 69. Of 90 negro skulls of various tribes, of the largest, 99; of the smallest, 68.

The smallest capacity, 53, is observed in the ancient Peruvians, and the largest, 114, in the Teutonic Family. Here is a wide difference, one brain being more than twice as large as the other. But the largest Peruvian skull has a capacity of 101; while the smallest Teuton has a capacity of 65, or a trifle more than half the former. The smallest negro skull has a capacity of 63, and the largest Tchudic 112.5, or almost twice as much; but the smallest Tchudic has but 81.5, while the largest negro has 99. These comparisons will suggest others, and it will be found that they yield like results when applied between all the families of mankind. There is as much variation in the capacity of skull, that is, size of brain, in any one race, as exists between the various races.

It has been said that animals of different species will not propagate; or, if they do, their offspring are unprolific. The mule offspring of the horse and ass is a familiar example. Until recently, it has never been disputed that all races of men were equally prolific when mingled together. The example of England, created out of different nations, and of the United States, made up of fragments of almost every race on the earth, are standing examples of the perfect blending of races. I say, until recently; for a class of writers have allied themselves, and prostituted science to the slave-power, and endeavored to prove that the offspring of the negro and white, after a few generations, inevitably perishes, showing, they think, a weakened constitution, or an imperfect power of propagation, the result of hybridity. Were it not for the counter facts which show the mulatto to be as long-lived and able to rear as large families as negroes or whites, it might be well asked if species must not be nearly allied to the closely related varieties, if the effect of hybridity on their offspring could escape the notice of all the world until wanted to prove the inferiority of the negro slave.

The statement, so often produced, that the Australian women are sterile to the males of their own race, after producing by Europeans, was first made by two credulous travellers, since repeatedly contradicted, but recently revived by pretenders to scientific knowledge.

It is unessential whether races be called species, or permanent varieties, or simply varieties: what I desire is to show the relationship of all races or varieties to be sufficiently intimate to prove their common parentage. The facts of this chapter point only to such a conclusion. The same tests have been applied as are employed to fix the position of species of animals, and their requirements have been fully complied with.

In duration of life, and the periodical functions of the system; in predisposition to contagious and epidemical diseases; in size and structure; in color of skin and hair; in capacity of skull, and in perfect prolificacy, *inter se,* — the races of men differ no more than species of any other genus of animals: they differ as much, and in precisely the same manner. They differ as the white bear differs from the brown, as the latter from the black, as the black from the bear of Europe, as the tiger differs from the lion, the lion from the panther or leopard. The difference is not in kind, but in degree.

It is thus seen that the races, varieties, types, or species of mankind are associated into one family, bound together by the ties of a common origin.

The objection is urged against this unity of parentage, that the delineations of races on the walls of Egyptian temples, made at least four thousand years ago, and probably nearer six thousand, preserve the expression of each, as well as the artists' crude method would allow, as they appear at present. The Copt, the Semite, the African, can all be perfectly identified. If, for four thousand or six thousand years, there has been no perceptible change, urges a certain school of ethnologists, are not the races permanent? and how did they ever originate from one another? Granting the Mosaic chronology to be correct, it is evident that the Egyptian paintings show a diversity which cannot be reconciled with a common origin. But science has been completely severed from theology. It has been shown that six thousand years is but a day since man was introduced. Hence a conclusion drawn from so short a period is untrustworthy, were the pictures known to be absolutely faithful.

From the known caricatures they have left, and their conventional, stereotyped manner, reliance cannot be placed in their outlines, sufficient to yield a scientific conclusion that there has been *no change.* All that can be said is, that they preserve the general expression of each race. Their pictures inform us of this sufficiently well, so as not to need explanation.

It so happens that the races depicted, the Semite and African, are the ones which have changed the least. They belong to the stationary races. It is probable that a picture of a Chinese three thousand years ago would be good for a Chinese to-day. The great change which yields the civilization of the present belongs to races wholly unknown to the Egyptians. That these have changed, and are daily changing, no observer can deny.

CHAPTER VI.

RELATION OF CONTINENTAL FORMS TO MAN.

Bacon's Observation. — Analogies between the Continents. — Typical Continental Form. — The Three Double Worlds. — Benefits conferred on Man by Contour of the Land. — Influence of Mountain Chains, and of Large Bodies of Water. — What is Acclimation? — Application of foregoing Principles.

BACON first observed that the two worlds, the Old and the New, while they widened into broad masses towards the north, narrowed and terminated in points towards the Antarctic Ocean. The learned companion of Capt. Cook, Foster, in his second circumnavigation of the globe, developed this observation into three generalizations on the structure of continents.

The first, that the southern points of all the continents are mountainous. These are termini of chains radiating from the interior, and abruptly broken off at the shores of the ocean. Thus America terminates in the rocky heights of Cape Horn, where the Andes, already broken, fall in high cliffs into the Antarctic Ocean; Africa, in the plateaux of table-mountains; Asia, in the peninsula of the Deccan, where the giant Ghauts form the rocky Cape Comorin; lastly, Australia presents the same character at Cape South-east of Tasmania.

A second analogy is, that the continents directly east of these southern extremities have a large island or group. East of Cape Horn are the Falklands; of Cape of Good Hope, Madagascar and volcanic islands; of the Deccan, Ceylon; of Australia, New Zealand.

A third resemblance is in configuration. On the western side of all of them, their flanks are, as it were, hollowed into a vast gulf. This inflection is indicated in America by the position of Arica at the foot of the high Cordilleras in Bolivia, in Africa by the Gulf of Cambay and the Indo-Persian Sea, in Australia by the Gulf of Nuyts.

It will be observed by a glance at the map of the world that all the masses of land widen as they extend northward. This is not only true of the principal masses, but of the smallest. Greenland, California, Florida, in the New World; Italy, Spain, Scandinavia, Greece, the two Indies, Corea, Kamtschatka, in the Old,—point southward, but conform to the above statement. Steffens brings to view that the land is grouped in three great masses, or double worlds, composed of two parts united by an isthmus or chain of islands, on one side of which is found an archipelago, and on the other side a peninsula.

The Americas are the type of this arrangement. The two parts, North and South America, are of about equal size, of similar form; and the Isthmus of Panama which unites them is perfect. On the east is the archipelago of the Antilles; on the west, the peninsula of California.

The two other double worlds are less perfectly defined, and symmetrical. Their component continents are of unequal size, and, as it were, turned back to back. They are united along the line of the Caucasus down to the Persian Gulf. Of the western double world, Europe, a part of Western Asia, and Arabia, are the northern part, united by the Isthmus of Suez with Africa, the southern counterpart. The western archipelago is Greece, the peninsula is Arabia. The eastern double world, Asia and Australia, approaches nearer the type. Asia is its northern part; the isthmus is broken into a chain of islands uniting it with Australia, the southern part: it possesses the great archipelagos of Borneo, Moluccas, and Celébes, and a peninsula, India, of vast extent.

Another aspect of configuration is of momentous consequence. The massing of land into great bodies is not favorable to civilization. Africa is the most solid of the continents, Europe the most intersected by the sea. The facilities of commerce, the variety of scenery, the stimulus imparted by natural divisions into nationalities, are broad themes, based not so much on the constitution of man as on that of the globe.

Such are a few leading resemblances between the great continents. In respect to the globe, other characters are equally well defined. A necessity of the present contour of the continents is the vast preponderance of land in the northern hemisphere.* The globe may be so divided that one-half is almost entirely covered by water, and the major portion of the other half by land. A circle drawn through the coast of Peru and the south of Asia so divides the earth

* First remarked by Ritter.

into a terrestrial and oceanic hemisphere. Then, in one of these halves, are grouped all the important masses of land, while in the vast ocean of the other only float scattered groups of islands and the extremities of the most projecting peninsulas, and Australia, the most insignificant of the continents.

In the grouping of the lands, the Old and New Worlds are the exact reverse. The masses in the Old World stretch from east to west; in the New, from north to south. One consequence of this arrangement, which at first appears of little moment, is that Asia and Europe have a vast area occupying the same zone; while America, traversing all the zones of the earth, presents a great variety of phenomena. As will be readily admitted, this configuration exerts a great influence on mankind, an influence hereafter to be more fully considered.

All the facts of Nature are dependent and mutually related. Thus the shape of continents, foreign as it appears to intellectual development, bears with great force, as will be hereafter shown, on its advancement.

The similarity of form in the three continental masses points to a law by which they were fashioned; and as man, the plastic being, must conform to the implastic conditions of the continents in order to be in harmony with their conditions, he becomes directly related to the laws by which they were produced.

Let us consider his relations to the country in which he is placed, and the results of slight differences of configuration. If the continents were depressed a few hundred feet, nothing would remain but the high table-lands and mountain summits above an almost universal ocean. An elevation of a few hundred feet would throw the continents up into the cold strata of the atmosphere, and transform the tropics into arctic regions. Such trivial causes decide whether a country shall be a torrid plain, a dry plateau, a desert of sand, a waste of water, or a fruitful plain. A few feet of elevation only makes the difference between the airy table-lands of Mexico, and the pestilential plains at its feet; between the fertile plains of India, and the cold, barren plateaux of Thibet.

For example, take North America; suppose it to be tilled so that its great rivers, instead of flowing into the Gulf of Mexico, empty into the Arctic Ocean: for the purposes of civilization, the continent would be a failure. Commerce could not flow to the north, and for its purposes the rivers would be useless. The lands facing the sweeping arctic winds would return a poor encouragement to agriculture; and nothing would be left to the unfortunate people who inhabited it but to become nomadic, and gain a scant subsistence from their wandering herds, like the people of Northern Asia, where precisely such conditions exist. Thus the direction of the inclination of continents, small as its influence would appear, exerts a vast power on civilization.

Glance for a moment at the influence exerted by mountain chains. Setting aside the barriers they oppose between the mingling of nationalities, hemming in ambitious communities, and protecting weaker tribes from the encroachments of stronger neighbors, their influence on climate alone is incalculable. Suppose the Rocky Mountains, instead of skirting the western shores of America, were placed in the position of the Great Lakes; protected from arctic winds, the countries to the south would perfectly represent the plains of India. The United States would be entirely free from the influence of the cold gales which are so severe in winter, in spring and autumn, and of which summer is not wholly free.

Still greater would be the changes were the Andes placed on the eastern instead of the western coast of South America. Now, the trade-winds deluge the vast plains of Brazil, pouring torrents on the very summit of that range, creating the largest rivers on the globe, — the La Platte, Orinoco, and Amazon, the latter one hundred and fifty miles broad at its mouth, and pouring a torrent of such strength as to combat successfully with the tides of the sea. But, as the winds pass over, their last drop of moisture is wrung from them, and the narrow belt of land between them and the Pacific is nearly or quite rainless: the condition which would prevail over the whole continent were the Andes placed on the eastern instead of the western coast of South America; and, like the rainless regions of Peru and Chili, not a rain-drop would fall on the illimitable expanse of desert, nor a cloud obscure the burning expanse of its sky.

Taking the world as it is, we see that physical conditions determine the variety of men who permanently occupy any given region.

The occupying race have been brought into equilibrium with those conditions at some indefinite time in the past, and now, so to speak, being acclimated, hold it against all others; for climate, which is their safeguard, is destructive to a foreign people. In the earliest historic epoch, this equilibrium had become well established. Each race held essentially the same countries as at present. The Semite, the Negro, the European, each held the same provinces as now. The people of Arabia, of Northern Africa, of the Steppes of Asia, tended their herds, and roamed over the wastes, in the same manner as they do to-day. Civilization can never rise above the pastoral state in those countries; for, to its high advancement, there must be a crowded population and an abundance of food. In countries so barren that but a family can exist to the square mile, little progress can occur. The deserts must always be peopled by nomads; and the fertile plains, by dense agricultural populations.

There are climates where no human being can exist, as that of the celebrated Campagna and Pontine, which affects the Italian just as it did in the days of Livy. Those who are compelled to dwell in the poisonous district, show, by their bloated forms, distorted features, dark-yellow complexion, and livid lips, that there is no acclimation against such a climate. Generally, however, some races are more affected than others. The African seems perfectly acclimated to all torrid climates, and able to bear, unharmed, vicissitudes which are wholly insupportable by lighter races. When transported to the low seaboard lands of the Southern States, they not only enjoy health, but rapidly increase, and attain a remarkable longevity; while the European, avoiding every exposure, and occupying the healthiest localities, from earliest infancy manifests symptoms of the insidious working of the malarious influence which early disorganizes the human fabric. The negro labors in the rice-swamp all day beneath the burning sun, without danger; but a single hour's exposure of the European often so impregnates the morbific matter, that no medicine can alleviate its rapid progress to dissolution. Chemistry cannot detect the character of the malaria; for it is extremely subtle, and powerful in proportion to its subtlety. It does not result always from decomposition of animal or vegetable matter alone. The Campagna does not differ from other plains; nor does the deadly vicinity of Vera Cruz, with its long stretch of sandy beach and sand-hills, differ from other shores. Such decompositions may assist; but to them must be added direct exhalations from the earth, the cause of which we do not understand.

From the yellow fever the negro is exempt, or nearly so,—his liability to it has been determined as 13.19 to 6000.4,—and he escapes the deadly malaria of Vera Cruz.

The same holds good between the Oceanicans and the cinnamon-colored Polynesians. The Island of Vanikow has a climate so deadly to the latter, that a night's exposure is certain death; but the former enjoy perfect health. Some regions of Hindostan are so deadly, that they cannot be visited by whites; but the Hindoo inhabits them, enjoys health, and lives to a good age.

Such are a few of the leading facts adduced to prove that the races of men are primordially distinct, and are here brought forward to show that they do not point in that direction: all that can be claimed for them is, that they refer to races as they are, not as they have been; they do not prove the impossibility of acclimation, but the vast period requisite to bring about an equilibrium between man and a given province. The African cannot go north, on account of liability to consumption, scrofula, and kindred diseases, as well as the white can go south. The freedom from malarious influences appears to be in proportion to the darkness of color; even dark-skinned brunettes bearing more exposure than blondes. This should be so; for is not the darkness of skin an index of acclimation?

The application of these considerations is easily made. If we suppose Central Asia to be the point of dispersion, the waves of emigration must necessarily follow the paths marked out by the geographical contour of the surrounding lands. When the earliest waves set out, they were rudest savages, without even a bow and arrow. They could not pass broad rivers, arms of the sea, or mountain chains. They were walled in by these.

Had the Old World been one vast and interminable plain, the dispersion of man had been quite different. There had been but little of that difference of race now so notable, the differentiation of continental masses having direct influence on the differentiation of race.

If the map of Asia be examined, it will be seen that to a point south-east of the Caspian Sea, or towards the Highlands of Toorkistan, all the great mountain chains converge. Although hemmed in by lofty mountains, there are gateways left on every side, through which emigration can readily pass. Between the Black Sea and the Caspian, such a passage exists, leading into Europe: although closed by the Caucasus Mountains, it has many easy passes, and affords a ready entrance into Europe. Through this passage emigrated the Finns, Iberians, the Celts, and Aryans, or Indo-Europeans.

Between the Caspian and Persian Gulf, another passage exists into Arabia, and, beyond the Isthmus of Suez, leads into the vast continent of Africa.

The Ural Mountains prevented the Turanian or Mongolic waves from overflowing Europe, throwing them off to the north and east, while the Himalaya confined them on the south: the latter chain protected the commingling of the Dravidians, and latterly the Aryans, who were thrown south of that range in Hindostan, passing into those interminable plains over the sources of the Indus. Had the Red Sea communicated with the Mediterranean, Africa would have remained uninhabited for an indeterminable time, and would not have been peopled until man had learned the art of navigation. Had the gateway of the Caucasus been closed, and the Indo-Europeans forced north along the eastern side of the Ural Mountains, so as to enter Europe from the north, the arrested development shown in the Tungusic tribes would have resulted, and its civilization been no higher than those tribes present.

Such considerations might be indefinitely extended: they show the strict dependence of man on external nature.

The continents were first created, and then man. They do not harmonize with him; but he, as the plastic material, is compelled to conform to the accidents of his surroundings.

CHAPTER VII.

THE FIRST WAVES OF DISPERSION: THE ORIENTAL NEGRO, AFRICAN AND SEMITE.

The ORIENTAL NEGRO, or the Australian Race. — When originated the three Great Branches, SEMITIC, TURANIAN, ARYAN? — The SEMITIC. — Structure of Language; divided into Aramean, Hebrew, Arabian; Description of Character, Language and History of Each. — Nestorians. — Berbers. — Phœnicians. — Egyptians, Language of, Origin of, Shepherd Kings of. — Copts. — African Tribes of Semitic Origin: Haussa, Gallas, Berberins, Fellatah, Mandingoes, Yoloffs. — AFRICAN RACE. — Description of, Origin of. — Divided into two Great Families, KAFFER and HOTTENTOT. — Language of Africa. — The DAMARAS. — The KAFFER. — The HOTTENTOT. — Description of, Language of, and History of Each.

THE race of men who used the fossil arrows have entirely passed away from Europe. They, there, have no living representative; but in India, and the Islands of the South Sea, there exists a race of men who seem to be the Autochthons, the primitive race. Whether they are similar to those who used the flint arrows of the drift cannot be decided; but this is certain, that, between the employés of the arrows and this race none other has left remains. This race has undoubtedly changed during the vast interval, but presents us with a sample of the most primitive people known to have existed. It is an ethnological fossil. It is a black race, speaking the most barbarous and undeveloped languages. It inhabits portions of the vast plains south of the Himalayas, and extends southward into the sea, constituting the aboriginal inhabitants of Borneo, the Philippines, New-Guinea, Australia, Tasmania, and extends eastward to New-South-Wales.

The people of the Andaman Isles, though their language is allied to the Siamese, Owen considers the lowest of mankind. They are of diminutive stature; they have no agriculture, no garments, no families, no idea of deity, or a future state. Without dwellings or the capacity to construct them, in the interior wilderness of Borneo, they occupy the branches of trees. They were the aboriginals of the Sandwich Islands prior to the real Polynesians, having left traces of their vocabulary in the language of the latter. According to Dr. Foster, the inhabitants of Mallicollo, approach nearer the animal than any other. Their bodies are entirely covered with black and brown hair, their skulls so pressed backwards, and the cheek-bones so broad, the face so sooty, as to impart the most disagreeable aspect. They are a "small, nimble, slender, ill-favored set of men, who, of all men he ever saw, border the nearest upon the tribes of monkeys." Equally degraded are the inhabitants of Tauna and New-Caledonia.

In Australia, this race exists in what is styled a most degenerate form, but, perhaps, really superior to the common stock at its departure therefrom. Thinly spread over vast regions, if there were few causes for advancement, there were none for degeneracy; and it appears reasonable that the race has remained nearly stationary from immemorial time, until, in a recent period, they were brought in contact with the Polynesians. The Australian may be taken as the representative of the original black race of Hindostan. A description of him is a description of man as he was prior to two strata of superimposed races.

The hardy Dampier, in 1686, astonished at the appearance of the natives of Australia, wrote, "The inhabitants of this country are the most miserable in the world, — who have no houses, no skin garments, or sheep, or poultry, or fruits of the earth, — and, setting aside their human shape, they differ but little from brutes."

Another writer, Mr. Collins, has accurately given their appearance: "Their noses are flat, nostrils wide, eyes much sunken in their heads, and covered with thick eyebrows; their lips thick, and mouth extravagantly large. Many have very prominent jaws; and there was one man, who, but for the gift of speech might well have passed for an orang-outang. He was remarkably hairy; his arms of uncommon length; in his gait he was not perfectly upright."

A strip of bark tied around the loins is a sufficient raiment, and he lies down where night overtakes him, like a wild beast; or, at best, makes a lair of a few branches. He does not enter into the relations of family, or of clan. He prowls in the forest like a wild animal, making no provision for the morrow, having no object of worship, or thought of a future existence.

Some authors have disagreed from the received statement of the low estate of this race. Pickering states that the finest example of muscular strength, and classical mould of head, he saw among Australians. From the physical appearance occasionally observed in individuals, it is probable that there is a slight infusion of Malay blood; although this is not confirmed by their language, which has not a single Malay word. They appear to be not a strictly homogeneous race, but mixed.

The reports of those interested in the instruction of Australian children, made to the British Government, state that they surpass Europeans in those studies depending on the perceptive faculties, but deficient in those depending on abstraction, are, without doubt, overdrawn. It cannot be supposed that offspring of parents unable to count above three, or at most, above five, show the same aptitude as Europeans. Such a state of savageness excludes conquest, or migration in masses. The extension of such a people occurs in the same manner as the spread of animals,— by the increase of population pressing outward; and, as they met with no preoccupying race, they were at liberty to wander as far as they pleased.

We have seen that the Ibero-Finnic waves in Europe correspond to the Dravidian of Hindostan; the Indo-European, to the Hindoo. Does the race of the flint age in like manner correspond to the Oriental-black? Confined by impassable barriers, the former have perished, while the latter, extending to the isles of the wide ocean, have remained securely isolated. Analogy teaches that wave after wave was sent off to the west through the Caucasus, to the south through the Hindoo-Kosh; and that the status of these waves at any given age was the same; and, perhaps, on this primitive race is founded the traditions so beautifully embodied in the "Kalawala" of the Finns. Have not the same causes which have preserved in Australia the fauna of the Oolite, while the remainder of the earth underwent the changes of myriads of ages, resulting in several complete changes of organic beings, also preserved a fragmentary living fossil of the early age of mankind?

Subsequent to the spread of the autochthonic black race, the true African stock was probably detached and spread over Africa. This conclusion is based on analogy only; for the structure of the negro dialects has as yet afforded no certain evidence of their origin. They must belong, however, to the earlier branches thrown off from the great centre.

The separation of the SEMITIC, the TURANIAN, and the ARYAN branches of mankind, occurred in the remote ages of pre-traditionary time. On the theory that the lower race must have separated first, the truth of which will be so far as possible substantiated in future pages, the SEMITIC must have been first thrown off, and the other two branches have remained united for a considerable length of time thereafter.

They remained until, as is shown by their corresponding words, they had invented fixed habitations, and domesticated the ox, horse, sheep, goat, and dog.

Like three great rivers, these great families of mankind roll back into the misty past, and we can only see at last the dim lustre of their waves; but we can note their directions, and see that their converging lines meet beyond the clouds and fog which shut them from our view. Their divergence is far away, so remote that the structure of the languages of the streams, especially of the Aryan and Semitic are radically distinct, but by reducing words to their most radical forms, a marked resemblance is observed, enough to show a common origin.

As the earliest, we shall first speak of the SEMITIC Family. Setting aside anatomy, it is impossible to mistake a Semite; for his language is as unique as his physiognomy. All the branches of this family bear its indelible marks in the vital structure of their tongues, so prominent that the linguist is left in no doubt.

It differs from the other families of languages in the formation of its roots, which are composed of three consonants, while theirs is composed of one or two, linked with a vowel. It is consequently called tri-literal. Words are formed from these roots by varying the vowels, which are vague, and inserted between the rough consonants, or adding a syllable. Few words are formed by composition. The verb has but two tenses, the nouns but two genders, and case is in general not expressed by inflected forms. The structure of the sentence is simple, presenting none of the involutions of the Indo-European tongues. It has considerable poetic power, is expressive of passion and feeling, but is wanting in precision, and inadequate to express the mature results of thought. The pronunciation of its short words is jerking, and far from musical or elegant. But there is a rugged sublimity in its terse and ambiguous style, which sounds like the rude chant of the elements.

The SEMITES have the glory of producing the religious doctrines received by the most civilized races of the world. They have given the world three great religious systems, Judaism, Christianity, and Mohammedanism; and now the believers in their system of monotheism embrace all the civilized races of the world.

They have given the divine law to nations reaching the confines of the arctic circle, and those under the burning torrid; to the polished nations of Europe, and the hordes of the African deserts. Amid the surrounding mass of monstrous mythologies, and childish conjectures, they ever maintained the grand conception of one infinite, all-wise, and all-powerful God. He dwelt in light unapproachable, reflecting the stern and savage ideas of the Semite mind in his love for strict and unmitigated justice,—a justice terrible, vindictive, and revengeful. In the Old Testament or Koran, his image is the same.

If, however, he escaped prevailing mythologic ideas in regard to the unity of God, his sensuous and passionate mind invented mythological trappings environing that unity, which, becoming incorporated in Christianity, and flowing through the rank corruptions of Greece and Rome, concreted in the abominations of Romanism, and are plainly perceptible at the present.

The Semite attempted to build cities; but he was too restless to abide their completion. His religion bound him only long enough to build his temples. The Biblical account of the patriarchs tending their flocks on the great plains is true of Semitic life everywhere.

He loves traffic, connives at unlawful gain, has little energy, loves revenge, hates labor, is a cosmopolite;

the same three thousand years ago in his tent on the plains of Syria, the wastes of the desert, or selling clothes in the great metropolis ; austere, selfish, hating other races, with little that an Aryan would consider noble, or manly. Tenacious of the past, and disinclined to change, combining the strongest passions with the strongest religious sentiments, he is capable of astonishing acts of heroism, or rather fanaticism. A wandering people. The Arab in his tent is no more so than the dwellers at Jerusalem before its fall. They were always a dispersed people ; and now, although the moans of the Hebrews for the great and holy city is only equalled by the sighs of the Germans for their father-land, they may well be distrusted when, if they desired, they might purchase it with a tithe of what they possess.

The Semitic race is recognizable, most uniquely, through its negative characters: it has no mythology (of its own), "nor epopees ; neither science, nor philosophy ; neither fiction, nor plastic arts, nor civil life." No language has radiated less. It has always been confined in the peninsular space, between the Armenian mountains, and those which bound the basin of the Tigris ; and only by Phœnician colonization and Moslem invasion has it been partially dispersed.

The first emigrations of the Semitic race from Asia is lost even to tradition ; but twenty centuries B.C., Babylonian records show traces of Semitic forms. The geographical configuration of Asia indicates the great highways of these waves.

Supposing that the three great families of mankind sprang from Central Asia, the isolation of that portion known as Armenia and Mesopotamia, by the mountain barrier separating them from Persia, affords the key whereby we can solve the problem of the differentiation of the Semitic branch. While, on the other side of this barrier, the Turanian and Aryan families remained together, the Semitic, cut off from their influence, swept onward in a career emphatically its own, ages after to meet those families after they had passed the Caucasus and the Black Sea, on the shores of the Mediterranean. From their centre of dispersion at the foot of this barrier, they extended southward, along the western shores of the Persian Gulf, over all Arabia to the Gulf of Aden and the Arabian Sea, and westward over Asia Minor, clustering around the Mediterranean. By colonization, or pouring through the gate of the Isthmus of Suez, they extended along the southern coast of the Mediterranean, occupying the country from the sea to the desert, and breaking at length on the Atlantic shore, or extending even to the Canary Isles. The little known of the extinct Cannaries or Guanches showing that they were of the Berber race. Southward along the western shore of the Red Sea, they reached and occupied Abyssinia.

This wide dispersion created as wide a difference of dialects; yet small in comparison with the Turanian or Aryan: a fact accounted for by the uniformity of the regions over which they spread. They are divisible into three orders: *Arameans, Hebrews,* and *Arabians.* The *Arameans* occupied Syria at an early period, and after the Hamite dynasties held possession of Babylon. The Modern Chaldee is the direct descendant of their language, which in the first century was spoken from the Mediterranean to the Tigris. It was the native speech of Christ and the Apostles. In it the Targum was composed, and it continued to be the literary language of the Jews to the tenth century, and of the cities or empires of Ninevah and Babylon. The Hebrew order embraces the Jews, the Canaanites, and Phœnicians.

Carthage, so long the successful rival of Rome, was a Phœnician colony; but the Carthaginians, when they settled in Africa, found the Berber before them, belonging to the same family, but of older birth. The "shepherd kings" who conquered Egypt, and held it at least five hundred years, were of undoubted Semitic stock. As delineated on the most ancient monuments of Egypt, the Semite differs little from the type he bears at present. The Jew is of the most hardy race of history. A dispersed people at least four centuries B.C. (Knox, "Races of Men"), they have been persecuted and despised by all other races; yet they have thrived wherever they have taken up their abode. It is impossible to annihilate or change them. The statements of Pritchard are not authenticated by closer observations. The Jew of the torrid is darker than of the temperate, but, in every thing else except that superficial character, is a Jew. They increase in Sweden faster than the Christian population; in Algiers they are the only people able to maintain themselves; in Aden, the hottest place in the world, and in Cochin China, they appear to be unaffected by the climate.

The *Arabians* originally occupied the peninsula of Arabia. The Hicayaritic inscriptions record their ancient form of speech, showing how extremely remote was their origin; and, if we accept Renan's conclusions, before them Arabia supported a Hamite population. In those early days they colonized Abyssinia, where their language, the Geez, is preserved in sacred writings. They also extended over Northern Africa, where they still remain under the name of Berber, and, with the tenacity which ever characterized this people, they held the valleys of the Atlas against the Carthaginians, Romans, Bazantines, Vandals, and later the Arabs, none of whom have been able to absorb or destroy them. They were, in the eleventh century, pressed towards the desert; yet they hold a larger area than any other people in Africa,—an area stretching from the northern skirts of the Atlas south over the Great Desert to the regions of the Niger and the Soudan, and from Egypt to the Atlantic ocean. They were the Libyans of the ancients. The great commercial race of the deserts,— their traders uniting the unknown intérior with the Mediterranean,—and natural robbers, they form the greatest obstacle to travellers in penetrating that interior. Their language is directly descended from the ancient Libyan, and so uncorrupted that the bi-lingual inscriptions on the rocks of Northern Africa show not only the same idioms but many of the letters used by modern Berbers.

It is in recent times that the Arabians spread over Northern Africa; and, finding the climate very similar to that of Arabia, they became people of the soil. Amid this mixture of peoples an aggregation is observed. The Moors, or Berbers, living in cities, forming the merchants, farmers, and tradesmen; the

Arabs on the plains are the shepherds; the Kabalyls in the mountains are ferocious robbers, while the Bedouin defies all restraint, and turns his hand against all. These are united under the common bond of the Mohammedan faith.

The African Arab has been modified by climate, and his dialect has so changed that the true Arabian understands him with difficulty; but he disdains to borrow the idiom of the conquered people. He pitches his tent in the subdued country, but generally refuses to mingle with the natives of the soil. Lithe, agile, capable of superhuman endurance, impatient of control, a lover of the desert, a monotheist by nature, despising labor, a lover of gain, especially of unlawful seizure,—such is the Arab of antiquity, such is the Arab of to-day. Along the southern border of the desert, where the Berber, Arab, and Negro races meet, a complete gradation takes place. On many of the oases, as *Ashen*, says Bartle, the harsh Berber character is blended with the playfulness and darker color of the African. The Berber now roams with his flocks over the ruins of a splendid civilization. That civilization was of his own race, but he held the soil, while they colonized. They flourished and decayed in his midst, and are so completely forgotten that the relics of their former grandeur awaken in him not even curiosity.

History finds the Phœnicians at the height of power and civilization. They have the honor of inventing the phonetic alphabet, which at once sweeps away the tedious and ambiguous systems of hieroglyphic writing, and of which our own is simply a modification in characters. They were exclusively maritime, and the boldest mariners of the world. If tradition be received they sailed down the Red Sea, and, after circumnavigating Africa, returned through the Pillars of Hercules and the Mediterranean; a feat not again attempted until after the lapse of more than two thousand years. Even the stormy isles of the Northern Ocean were visited by their galleys in search of tin; and the remote Baltic was searched for amber. To them is referred the invention of glass, and their artificers astonished the ancients by their ingenuity. Insatiate traffickers, they conveyed the commodities of India, by way of the Red Sea and the deserts, to the people of the West.

Carthage arose at the expense of the mother country; and the conquests of Alexander, and especially his founding the great commercial centre of Alexandria, situated on the natural highway between the East and the West, ruined Phœnician commerce.

By the captivity of the Jews, Hebrew became mixed with Aramean, the language of Babylon, and submerged by the political ascendency of the latter, and of Syria, at last to be swept away by the Arabic, which, since the conquest in 636 A.D., has become the language of the whole country originally occupied by the Semitic race.

One important historical race has not yet submitted to classification, but shows a nearer alliance to the Semite than to any other branch. They are the Egyptians, who were the wonder and admiration of the ancients, and from whom Greece and Rome received the rudiments worked up into their charming mythology.

The Nestorians, a fragment of the Semitic family belonging to the Aramean branch, are found amid the mountains of Kurdistan, and the northwest province of Persia. They are an exception to the Semite, who never renounces his religion; they having, in the fifth century, embraced Christianity. Their ancient language was the same as that spoken by Christ; but their modern speech is mixed with Persian, Kurdish, and Turkish words. Their missionaries present the most wonderful examples of perseverance and devotion.

When thinly scattered, they are subject to the Kurds; but one tribe, the Tiaree, are as ferocious as the Kurds, and have preserved their independence.

They are strictly pastoral, and are slowly coming under Turkish rule. They are mostly serfs, and suffer from extreme poverty. They are generally handsome, with light complexion, and head with a marked cut of features resembling the Jews.

The origin of the Egyptians has been a problem creative of great confusion. Their language was of too early date to bear the impress of collateral branches, and is isolated except in the Semitic direction. Its structure is what grammarians would call an advance on the Semitic; but its noun and pronoun are entirely like that family of tongues, and is profuse in aspirates. It is to history and etymology we must look for a solution. Known to the ancients as Egyptians and Ethiopians, they are not only interesting for their wonderful civilization, but from its being the only great empire, except the colony of Carthage, that the African continent has produced. Much learning has been expended in the controversy whether the Egyptian was a negro or not, which grew out of loose expressions of classic authors. The necessity for such wordy and never-ending debates has been set aside by the recent explorations of the ruins of Egyptian tombs and temples. In the tombs* the entire nation, generation after generation, is preserved. The skulls of these innumerable mummies are entirely distinct from the negro races, approaching in a decided manner the type of the European. The hair of the mummies is not wooly, but long and *flowing*, and, when best preserved, of a brown color. There can be no reasonable doubt but the sculptures on the monuments of Egypt are faithful delineations. They have been preserved in all their pristine freshness. There the negro is admirably drawn, having wooly hair and jetty countenance; and beside him are placed the red Egyptian, and the Semite. Pritchard doubted their African origin, and referred them to the Hindoos of the Ganges, a theory quite as baseless. The Sanskrit has no affinity for the language of Egypt; and there is not the least evidence of any communication having taken place between the Nile and the Ganges, not even a legendary tale.

The argument afforded by caste, a unique system, but alike adopted by Hindostan and Egypt, has been swept away by the revelation recently made that the division of caste never existed in Egypt, — Niebuhr notwithstanding, — and that it has been recently introduced among the Hindoos.

A clue to the origin of the Egyptians is given by Hodgson, who considers the earliest people of Egypt to have been Berbers. Situated in a fertile country, and pressed together, they would advance faster than wandering tribes. Their position on the highway between Asia and Africa exposed them to repeated inundations. The Berber or perhaps a still earlier Semitic wave from Asia formed the under stratum. The modelling of this early type is finely shown by the artists on their monuments. They were always a mixed people, and their sculptures, at least of their ruling class, show predominance of Semitic blood, and of that variety known as Chaldean.

Egypt was for ages a battle-ground between Asiatic and African races. After attaining a high state of civilization, having finished her system of government, and perfected her architecturc, the shepherd-kings for five hundred years kept her stationary. After their overthrow, she continued her triumphant march; but the shepherds, who were probably wandering Semitic tribes, added greatly to her future prosperity by introducing the horse and several other domestic animals. Their long residence could not otherwise than leave a deep trace, by admixture of blood. Before their conquest, as well as after, the sculptures of Egyptian kings indicate Semitic origin. Together with these rulers, there is sculptured negro slaves; and captive Semites, with features still more indicative, and what has been styled the true Egyptian type, having flat and expressionless features, appear, coming up from the primitive stratum or earliest race.

A cursory examination of engravings from Egyptian

monuments clearly indicates a highly developed people, but one extremely mixed, and offering a perplexing study. Many of the sculptured heads are of pure Grecian mould, and clearly must have been related in some manner to Greece. We pass entirely into the land of conjecture; but it is not improbable that a branch of the Pelasgi penetrated and were incorporated with the autochthonic race.

The Copts are the direct descendants of the old Egyptians, and have preserved the lowest type of their sculpture.

The origin of the Egyptians has been invested with needless importance. Seen through the mist of classic description, they seem to absorb the entire ancient world, where comparatively they were but an insignificant people. Their civilization was wonderful, occurring as it did, surrounded by barbarism, but is dwarfed when compared with that of the present Indo-European. The great diversity of type exhibited by the hieroglyphic paintings reveal an extremely mixed race of Semites and negroes, with a basic population indicating remote Semitic origin.

These sculptures commence about 4000 B.C., when the hieroglyphics were already perfected. What occurred previously? Linguistic research is silent, and we must abide conclusions drawn from monumental records.

There are many tribes in Africa north of the Mountains of the Moon, who, from their black color, have been classed with negroes. If reliance be placed in the affinities of language to determine the place the various tribes occupy in the classification of mankind, these peoples belong to the Semitic race, or to what some have called Hamitic, which is nothing more than an imaginary early branch of that race.

From the Berber of the coast of the Mediterranean, as we pass across the Desert of Sahara: the type changes almost insensibly from the Semitic to the Negro. There can be no doubt that this is the result of mixture of these races. Such blendings are observable in the Turanian fragment occupying the country between Lakes Yeou and Tsad, where the Berber element is added, and the inhabitants of the eastern part of the Great Desert, the Tibboo, who have elegant European features, with jetty black color, and speak a language allied to the ruling tribe of Borneo.

The Haussa occupy the centre of the continent and one of its finest provinces; and, until the beginning of this century, they held an important empire. They speak the Haussas, a tongue strongly Semitic. Their forms are graceful; their features regular, noble, and pleasing; and their temper lively, spirited, and cheerful. The Eastern Nubians are a very ancient people, who speak a language classed by Renan with the Semitic. Their physical type is neither Semitic nor Negro. They have regular European features, a dark or black countenance, and curly hair. They are a shrewd, energetic people, living a nomadic life.

Encircling Abyssinia, south of the Hamitic people of the Nile, are the *Gallas*, a people speaking a language thoroughly Semitic, and so powerful and warlike that they constantly encroach on the Abyssinians. They are a tall and well-formed people, with large foreheads, aquiline nose, well-cut mouth, a coppery color, and curly hair. They are the most infamous of all the slave-dealing tribes, and are extremely savage, delighting in drinking blood as it flows from the living animal; and some of their tribes do not even bury their dead, leaving them exposed, to be devoured by wild animals.

The high mountain plateau of Sennaar is inhabited by a race of a dark-brown color, frizzled hair, but regular features. They are classed by Renan as Semitic.

The *Berberins* of Nubia are described by Dénon as of a jetty-black color, exactly like that of antique bronzes, but without the smallest resemblance otherwise to the negro; their eyes deep-set and sparkling, with overhanging brows, high pointed nose, mouth wide, lips moderately thick. Their color is not always black, but is often coppery-red. Their face is perfectly oval, and nose often Grecian; their hair bushy, but not woolly. They are of precisely the Hamitic type, but their language cannot be assigned at present to any family.

The Fellatahs are a race inhabiting a territory equal in extent to one-tenth of Europe, extending from the Atlantic Ocean to Borneo on the east, from the Great Desert to the Bight of Benin and Kong Mountains on the south. They are of perfect European features, of a mahogany color, sometimes not darker than the Spaniard, and their hair straight. They have a noble bearing, are intelligent, and possess a deep poetic feeling, and are subject to the deepest enthusiasm. They are a nomadic people, who have made considerable advance in agriculture. They have lately attracted attention by the zeal they have displayed in promulgating the faith of Mohammed. In this they rival the Arab, and seem destined to extend the religion of the prophet over Africa. They are thus working a great change for the better; for it must be acknowledged that Mohammedanism is the best system which the African will receive, and that it is immeasurably superior to the fetichism of the negro. It prohibits human sacrifice, nourishes learning, and induces a belief in personal dignity, a trust in Providence, and unites all believers into a common brotherhood. It has also prevented the slave-trade. This is shown by the Fellatahs never having participated in the slave-trade, for, according to the Koran, a believer cannot become a slave.

Although greatly mixed, it is the opinion of those best qualified to judge that they are of the original Egyptian or Hamitic stock. Their language is primitive, and without an alphabet, and its numerals reach only five. It has a relationship in its alliteral changes to the Kaffer tongue, which probably is a degraded offspring of the primitive Hamito-Semitic. Its structure is allied to the Ashanti and Timmanee. The Mandingoes and Yoloffs on the Gambia and Senegal retain a vestige of Semitic blood largely diluted with the true African. They are zealous Mohammedans, but still are fetich in their worship. They possess well-ordered governments, and good public schools; and all their leading men can read and write Arabic. They are good agriculturists, and skilful manufacturers of cloth, leather, iron instruments, and their merchants enterprisingly conduct the principal commerce of Northern Africa.

The African, or negro, race, as will be seen by reference to the chart, were an early branch thrown off previous to the subdivision of the main stem into the other three great families. From this it will be understood that we are not to consider one race as springing from another, but each advancing after its own type in a parallel or diverging course.

The popular idea of the negro race, as sooty black, with woolly hair, flat noses, and long heels, is very erroneous, but has been countenanced by scientific works. This description applies only as a type, but is never fully realized.

There is no family of mankind among whom greater diversity exists than the African, as will be seen by a review of its various tribes. Some nations, as the Yoloffs, present the finest European forms, regular and perfect features, but their color is deepest black; while the people of the Gold Coast have perfect negro features, but are light colored. The Barabras and Bedjas present scarcely any other African peculiarity than a swarthy complexion, and curly hair. Other tribes have negro features, and black color, but straight hair. The Bechuana Kaffers have European features and form, and a light color, but woolly hair. Thus, through every gradation of hair, color, and features,— from the highest Aryan to the lowest Hottentot, — there are all grades, from woolly to straight, from white to black, from high, aquiline features to the depressed of the typical negro.

What is called the "negro type" is the exception, and seems to be the result of adverse circumstances. More than a general view of the innumerable tribes of Africa will not be profitable. It is of little avail to read lists of unpronounceable names. We can group the primary facts and thus render them available; but the countless negro tribes and dialects, the rise and fall of which counts in the progress of mankind scarcely more than the births and deaths of antelopes and lions of that locality, are of little use. The desert tribes, including all those dwelling north of the Mountains of the Moon, have been referred to elsewhere, as they show closer alliance to another branch, the Semitic or Hamito-Semitic.

It appears that a branch, marked in the chart as African, was thrown off at a very early period, and occupied Africa. When the Semitic wave bore the Berber, the Egyptian, and the Arab, successively to Africa, and perhaps a still earlier people, the two races, the African and Semitic, blended together. I have purposely arranged the tribes north of the Mountains of the Moon in a descending series, from the pure Semite to the almost African Mandingoe. It will be seen by the present chapter that the degradation can be carried still further. The Mandingoes are remarkable for their fine physique, and ingenuity in arts and agriculture; but in the dense jungles and swamps which line their coast for hundreds of miles, they assume what has been considered the true "negro type." The climate, deadly to Europeans, has exerted a moulding influence. We speak of Senegambia, which is peopled by a jetty black negro race. Northern Guinea is peopled by a low negro race, who are the most degraded pagans.

The tribes of the Gold Coast are more intelligent.

The Kons dwell on the coast from St. Andrew to Cape Mensurado. They have a fine physique, are of every grade of color, but have negro features. The Ashanti races have an inferior physical development, and do not present open or manly countenances. They have been exposed to the terrible blight of slavery; but missionaries have begun a civilizing process, which may reach high results.

The tribes of Benin, Dahomey, and Yoruba, have also been disorganized by the demand for slaves. Dahomey has become almost proverbially known. The people of Yoruba have a constitutional government, profess a monotheistic religion, are industrious, and notably free from licentiousness, and skilful in the arts.

All the northern tribes, even those which are absolutely "negro," have various religious customs which point to their Semitic parentage: "Such as circumcision; division of tribes into families, and often into the number twelve; the interdiction of marriage between families too nearly related; bloody sacrifices, and the sprinkling of blood upon the altars and doorposts; the observance of new moons, and weekly festivals; the division of time into seven days; the shaving the head, and wearing tattered clothes in sign of mourning; the rites of purification, and the belief in demoniacal possession."

One custom, however, is decidedly African: the heirship of all property descending to the females instead of the males, and through the sister instead of the son.

From the Mountains of the Moon south to the Southern Sea, the entire continent of Africa, from ocean to ocean, is peopled by a pure race of negroes, who have completely penetrated its every recess, and made it for immemorial ages their home. Their language proves them to be a unit, but throws no light on their origin, except it be to prove them to be a distinct people. It is not to be understood that a uniform type prevails. On the contrary, there exists the greatest diversity, from the high features of the European to the flat nose of the negro, and from jetty black to light yellow. The prominent nationalities which may be taken as characteristic of the countless inferior tribes, are the Pongo and Congo peoples of the Atlantic coast; the Kaffers, Zulucs, and Bechuanas of the south; the Swahere of the eastern coast; and the Hottentot Family. Thus the South-African tribes are divided into two great families, the Kaffers and Hottentots.

The latter are the oldest people, and probably inhabited the regions to the north, and were expelled southward by the approach of the Kaffers, a process still taking place. They would then appear as a contemporary wave of the oriental negro, whom they resemble. The Kaffers, who have given their name to the great North-African family, are a tall, robust race, with a deep black, or bronze, complexion. Their faces are oval, nose not depressed, and the hair only crisped. They are a pastoral and patriarchal people. Their language is soft and euphonious, but has incorporated the "click" of the Hottentot.

All the dialects of this family are distinguished by "alliteration," by which is meant that the "initial letter of the leading noun reappears in the beginning of all dependent or related words in the sentence."

Everything is sacrificed to this, as we often see in children's prattle, which it exactly resembles. As though a child should say, for, I am very thirsty to-day, Ti tam tvery thirsty to-tday. Nothing can show with greater force than this peculiarity the common origin of the tribes who use this strange euphony. The people of Southern Guinea all speak a Kaffer dialect, of which it is said, "there are perhaps no languages in the world capable of more definiteness and precision of expression."

The Damaras are supposed to have emigrated from the interior of Africa to the country they used to occupy, extending east from the Atlantic to Lake Ngami, within the last century. They are a pastoral people. They practise circumcision, and offer prayers and sacrifices to the spirit of the dead. They are in constant warfare with the Hottentots, whose territory they have invaded, and being rapidly exterminated. The Ovampas dwell to the north of the Damaras. They are skilled in working metals, in agriculture, and in commerce. Their love of country is so great that they are unprofitable for slaves, as they die of home-sickness.

The Bechuanas are the most powerful of the Kaffer races. They are keen wits, of revengeful temper, and given to theft. Agriculture flourishes under the care of the women, while the men engage in hunting and war. Their language is poor in abstract terms, having no words for conscience, spirit, &c., and hence their mental advance must be extremely limited.

The peoples of the eastern coast are more degraded than those of the western. They believe in the grossest fetichism, and are preyed upon by the most loathsome superstitions. They have felt also the blight of the slave-trade; and the most cruel and devastating wars have been waged for the purpose of slave capture.

The tribes of Kaffers are not stationary, but their state of unrest resembles that of the Germans in the first centuries. Gigantic emigrations *en masse* are constantly occurring, and nations are as constantly absorbed, conquered, or blotted out. The *Matabele* on the east have founded a vast empire, embracing many disjointed fragments; the Tschobe have erected another; and the Makalolo have nearly perished by fever. The emigration of the Damaras has already been spoken of, and also that they were rapidly perishing by the fierce onslaughts of Hottentot tribes.

THE HOTTENTOT. I stated that this is the oldest African family. That it extended far to the north is shown by the Hottentot names the rivers in the Kaffer country still retain, and also by fragments of tribes which dwell as far north, and even beyond, Lake Ngami. In the deserts, where the most degraded Kaffer tribes live by the side of the Bushman, the vitality of race is beautifully shown. They have lived thus for ages, but are as distinct as when they first came in contact. The former will grow pumpkins, and keep a few goats; but the latter know nothing of even such little arts, and lead a brutal life, depending for subsistence on the scanty game and vermin of the desert.

The Hottentots have been pushed southward until

they have reached the extremity of Africa. Here they recently met a new pressure. The European Cape Colony began driving them back against their old enemies; and between the two forces they are rapidly declining. The whole number of pure Hottentots is not estimated to exceed 20,000.

Other tribes on the south-western coast have disappeared, and others have mingled with the whites, producing a mongrel race called Griquas. The Bushmen, or Bosjesmen are the most remarkable of the Hottentot tribes. It has been supposed that they were merely degraded members of that people; but their independent dialect shows them to be distinct, and they are now supposed to be the earliest wave of that people who entered Southern Africa, and, as the Turanians were beaten down by the Aryans in India, so they were oppressed by the succeeding Hottentots. A deadly hatred still exists between them. The territory of the Cape Colony was the central abode of the Bushmen. They had been pushed to the very brink of the Continent. They are in the most savage condition, living in burrows or bushes. Yet, savage as they are, they are excellent herdsmen, in the employ of the colonists, and the only African race that has manifested any aptitude for art, the only race who have sought to express ideas by rude carvings on rock and tree. Fragments of this people dwell as far north as Lake Ngami, and it is thought, from the slaves brought from the interior of Africa, that they may be scattered over all South Africa.

Their moral condition is the lowest. They have no

family ties, nor personal names; no name for wife. They are cheerful, friendly, and true to their promise.

The descriptions of the Bushmen have been drawn from the most exaggerated examples. They often present fair proportions; but they are usually badly fed, and often suffer the most pinching want. Small ground-animals, as rats and mice, are their staple food; and they wander over the deserts of the Great South Namaqua-land where there are only four inhabitants to a square mile. Hence they present a dwarfish size, sometimes less than five feet, with thin limbs, slight body, and projecting abdomen. Their high and prominent cheek-bones, oblique eyes, flat noses, and yellow skin give them a decided Mongolian expression. Their skull is narrow and long, the hair grows in tufts, leaving bare spaces between, and, when long, hangs in knotted curls like pipe-stems.

Their language is distinguished by "deep, aspirated gutterals, harsh consonants, and a multitude of ugly, inimitable clicks." Yet its structure, in grammatical gender and accusative case, allies it to the most highly organized languages. Its affinities are with Coptic and Semitic. This fact is illustrated in the chart, by placing them next to those races. These points of resemblance between the earliest peoples, however indistinct, are extremely interesting, as they point unmistakably to the original unity of the races so allied.

Our survey of the African tribes has been very brief, nor does it appear necessary to dwell on the minute descriptions of people whose names perhaps will be for the first time presented, and in an hour will be forgotten; who have no part in our civilization, and little in that of the world. All the facts which go towards illustrating the origin of races which they afford will be used in appropriate order; and that is all the service that can be wrung from them.

CHAPTER VIII.

THE NORTH TURANIAN RACES.

Name, Derivation of. —Which are the Autochthonic, the Aborignal Races ?— Wide extent of the Turanian Family. — Characteristics of Languages, Agglutination.— Successive Waves. — The Chinese.— Iberians.— Lapps. — Finns.— Permians.— Votiaks.— Tscheremisses. — Voguls. — Ostiaks, &c. — Samoiedes. — The Mongolians. — Turkish Race. — Turkomans.— Usbeks. — Kirgis. — Yakuts. — The TUNGUSIANS. — Mandshus. — Ostiaks of the Yenisei. — Yakagers. — Kamtschadales. — Aino. — Coreans. — Japanese.— Lew-Chew Islanders.— American Indians, Similarity of.— Unity of, Origin of. — Origin of Indian Tribes. — The INCAS and AZTECS, from whence Derived. — Relations between the Indians and Northern Asiatics. — The Destiny of the Red Race. — Turanians of the Caucasus: GEORGIANS, CIRCASSIANS, ABYSSINIANS.

THE great stem from which the Semitic branch sprang continued united with the parent trunk for a length of time thereafter, as shown by the closer relationship of the languages thus continuing together. This relationship is so evident, that high authorities have said that there were really but two families of languages, — the SEMITIC and ARYAN; thus confounding the Turanian with the latter.

We must not be misled by classification, which is imperfect and arbitrary at best. In the early days of their separation, mixtures would occur; and we find, that, faintly as the line is drawn between the blending members of Semitic and Turanian, that between Turanian and Aryan is still less perceptible.

The name of this great family is derived from Tura, the swiftness of the horse: it being applied by the Aryans to the barbarous country lying outside of their own. They are widely spread; and so remotely have their branches diverged that only by the closest attention to analogy can their relations be determined. The difficulties which environ the subject are increased by the blending of nationalities, by which their salient characters are, more or less, obliterated; and, as the dispersion occurred countless ages before the most vague record, it is in vain we look for aid to history. Should we successfully account for the origin of the existing races, still there remain extinct races, — not autochthonic, for we have seen that people after people have succeeded each other, leaving only vestiges of their existence in many places scattered over the globe. Of these we can only conjecture that they were waves thrown off in vastly remote ages from some creative centre. Of these we learn by remnants driven into mountain fastnesses by the predominance of superior races, where they have maintained their purity by isolation. These relics are the ancient types of the vast Turanian family which now, here and there, over the whole of the Old World, crop out, like the mountain-cliffs to which they have been driven, through the thick strata of other nationalities. They are the oldest people of which we can learn by the study of language. Undoubtedly, between them and the employés of the flint arrows of the Drift numberless others existed, stratum on stratum. But of them we can only conjecture, and by imagination bridge the vast interval.

The study and classification of the Turanian tongues has been the grandest triumph of comparative philology. The fact that the structure of savage languages is more intricate, and hence their affinities more strongly marked, has been of great assistance. Embracing the wandering tribes from the North Cape to the Pacific Ocean, the Chinese, the Dravidian-Hindoo, the Malay and Polynesian, and the entire Indian people of the New World, its limits are at once strongly marked and imperceptibly blended. It embraces at least two-thirds of mankind, forming the understratum, and savage element, at no time or place attaining any great civilization. Its languages have been styled Nomadic from the wandering character of this family, and the great fluctuations which occur in themselves. They are characterized by agglutination, or the building up of phrases by *gluing* word to word, so that the phrase is but a single word. They are also distinguished for the regularity of their forms; the indiscriminate use of the same word as noun, adjective, and verb; and the rapid divergence made by these dialects, resulting from the isolated tribes wandering over vast plains; and absence of written forms. It must be remembered, that, previous to their separation, the Aryan and Turanian branches spoke the same primitive language. The agglutinized form is necessarily the earliest effort of the mind to express its thoughts.

Müller separates the Turanians into two divisions, — the northern and southern. The former includes the Tungusic, Mongolic, Turkic, Samoiedic, and Finnic classes; the latter the Taïc, Malaic, Gangetic, Lohitic,

Munda, and Tamulic. To the northern division the American Indian may be added.

It is entirely by the comparative study of their languages that he supposes there were two directions for their migration, north and south, from the table-lands of Central Asia. The first southern wave — the Taïc — settled on the Meikong, Meinam, Irrawaddy, and Brahmapootra; the first northern, on the Amoor and Lena, founding the Tungusic tribes. A second to the south pushed on to the islands of the South Sea, and founded the Malays; a third poured through the Himalaya, and formed the original native population of India, crushed by the conquering Aryan-Hindoos. A second to the north originated the Mongul; and a third, the Turkish tribes. This is only an hypothesis which can never be proved. The number and direction of these emigrations can never be known. According to Rawlinson, the enthusiastic decipherer of the inscriptions of Nineveh, the "Median Empire," which flourished and fell before Nineveh was known, 2458 - 2234 B. C., was composed of a mixture of Turanian races with Semitic or Egyptian. Even then, the Chinese Empire was as glorious as to-day. Remotely situated from the arena of classic history, its existence was unknown.

From the *infantile* structure of the Chinese language, together with the discovery that, at least 2000 B.C., they had a fixed and permanent government, they are supposed to be the earliest crystallization of the Turanian race. Chinese is distinguished by its *singing* accent, which designates the word, and remains absolutely fixed; for, if it changes in the slightest degree, it produces a new word. A departure is observed in the Siamese, in laying the stress on the last word of a compound expression. The Burman takes a conspicuous step towards agglutination, which is seen more decidedly in the Thibetan, which is furthest separated from the monosyllabic tongues.

It has no grammar, as we understand that word; that is, no inflections or declensions; but the relations of words entirely depend on their localities in the sentence. Its words are all roots, having never been changed by prefixes or suffixes, thus remaining in the most primitive possible state. Although more civilized than other members of this family, the language is the most undeveloped of all. They have advanced to the agglutinative stage, but the Chinese presents but slight approach to this more progressed form. Yet we must allow that these agglutinative tongues were once as simple as the Chinese. By some fatality, and probably by its early fixture in the sacred writings of Confucius, the latter has remained almost immovable.

The twelve thousand characters or letters in this language were once the pictures of the objects they represent, but now contracted into seemingly arbitrary signs. All its characters are such contractions of pictures once used, and, as the contraction is not governed by any rule, and it is not allowable to introduce a new picture for a word, how can a new idea be expressed?

The labor of learning these characters, to use them correctly, and write them elegantly, comprises the tedious system of Chinese education, on the success of which all preferment depends. If an idea is to be expressed, it must be written exactly after the pattern furnished by the classics, and hence must become the same idea. A better plan to fetter and stagnate thought cannot be conceived. There can be no literary progress until the whole system is thrown aside for a phonetic alphabet, an event which will not occur until forced on them by a conquering race. With such a clumsy method, poetry and oratory cannot flourish, though all the poetry and fire of *Chinese* character, perhaps, can be expressed. The affinities of their dialect have not been considered sufficiently explicit to place the Chinese in the Turanian family; but whatever evidence is thus furnished is supported by physical characters. The obliquity of the eyelids and smallness of the eyes, the lank, straight, black hair, and yellow color, point in the same direction as linguistic alliances. The Mandshus are superior to the Chinese proper, being more warlike, and better capable of ruling.

Turanian fragments exist in Europe, as previously stated. Of these, the IBERIANS have attracted great attention from the anomaly of the *Basque* language which they speak. It is preëminently agglutinative, and strikingly related to the languages of America. It compares the idea-word, and, in so doing, suppresses entire syllables, presenting sometimes only a single letter of a root, and distinguishes case by the striking use of post-positions. It is similar to the Tartar tongues, to which Finnic makes a closer approach.

So isolated have they remained in their mountain

fastnesses that they seem like a foreign people dropped into the centre of Europe. According to Strabo, they were not originally warlike; were moderately endowed with natural gifts; were a laborious, agricultural, and mining race, until driven by the inundation of the Celtic Gauls into the fastnesses of the Pyrenees, and, by the bruises of war, compelled to defend themselves. There they have remained, their jealousy of each other preventing the petty tribes into which they are divided from uniting, even sufficiently to maintain their independence. From their abhorrence of foreigners they have remained comparatively pure, a fossil people, from an age immensely remote from the ken of history. They have retained, on their poor soil, their love of agriculture, and are still miners. Their costumes, dances, and amusements are like those of their immemorial ancestors, as is their extreme affection for their dead.

Ancient writers mention them as having arrived at a remarkable degree of civilization. They were noted for their success in mining, and were widely dispersed, even to the islands of Corsica and Sardinia. They had been several times invaded by Celtic tribes, who forced themselves over the Pyrenees, and were eventually almost annihilated.

From the traces left of allied tribes, it appears that the Iberians, Finns, and Lapps entered Europe from the north and east. Whether to them the rude remains of works of art so abundantly scattered are to be referred is a question of doubt. Some of the latter, mounds, piles of huge blocks of stone, and the lake-dwellings of Switzerland may, with high probability, be referred to them.

The mountains saved the Iberians; their inhospitable climate, the Lapps and Finns. Crowded to the north, until they reached a land where the harvest was too unpromising to invite further pursuit, the severity of climate has told destructively on the Lapps; so much so, that they are the lowest people of Europe. No instance better shows the effect of climate than the contrast presented between them and the Magyars. The former have a dusky complexion, scanty beard, protruding chin, high cheek-bones, slender limbs, oblique eyes; in short, are the most unsightly of the tribes of Europe; the latter are the most symmetrically formed, being models of physical perfection, and only by an occasional obliquity of the eyelids do they denote their descension from the Ostiaks, as ugly and disgusting as the Lapps. They are the only nomadic and heathen population of Europe. They have their reindeer and dogs, — their only domestic animals, — and their locality is determined by pasturage.

The FINNS are not inferior in physical development. Their complexion is dusky, and they have a serious and gloomy expression, with a strong tendency to superstition, and hence by nature lovers of the subterranean regions of mines. Wilful and morose, they do not change their own ways, nor learn those of strangers.

While the other Turanian dialects have been in a great measure adulterated by wars, and blendings with other peoples, the Finnic has, by isolation and early embodiment in sacred songs, been preserved in purity. The Finns are one of the best-cultivated of the Turanian races, and to them belongs the honor of producing and transmitting the *Kalawala*, one of the few great epic poems of the world, and almost the only one produced by the Turanian race.

Europe has received great benefit from the Hungarians or Magyars. They have taught how to organize a constitutional government, which gives great liberties to subjects, yet holds them amenable to law. They also taught courtesy and dignity of manners. Their origin is proved by their language to be held in common with the Finns, Lapps,* and the Ostiaks who inhabit Bashkiria, situated at the northern extremity of the Ural Mountains, through the passes of which they came from Asia.

The Permians, Votiaks, Tscheremisses, Voguls, Ostiaks, are some of the principal tribes that inhabit the countries watered by the Vishera, Viatka, Kama, Obi, Irtish, and the Uralian chain, the dialects of all of whom are allied to the Finnic.

The *Samoiedes* are a race dwelling on the shores of the Frozen Ocean, and extending up the great rivers from the Gulf of Kara to Yenisei.

They have a few reindeer, but subsist by hunting, and devour dead whales and marine animals that drift ashore. It has been found that traces of this people exist in the south of Siberia, and they appear to have been crowded towards the north, as the Lapps have been in Europe. Their traditions say that they came from Eastern countries.

The dialects of the Samoiedes are closely allied

* Strahlenberg, Ruysbroek.

and are united with the Tschudic or Finnic and the Caucasian. The latter fact points to the time when they passed through the gates of the Caucasian Mountains.

The Mongolian race is divisible into the Mongols proper, the Buriats, and the Kalmucks. The Mongols have been taken as representatives or types of the Turanian race, but do not represent it as well as some others. The countries around the Altai Mountains, especially to the north, have from immemorial time been the home of these people, the lakes, mountains, and rivers retaining the names given by them.

The Mongols are nomads, and inhabit Mongolia, a great steppe or plain north of China, and are scattered in Siberia. They are now ruled by governments they once overthrew. They are timid and credulous, but terrible when excited by vengeance or fanaticism.

The Buriats wander in Siberia from the border of China to the Upper Lena.

The Kalmucks' native country is the mountainous region on the frontier of Turkestan and China, but colonies have wandered to the Don and Volga, and into Siberia. They have high, prominent, and broad cheek-bones; small eyes, widely separated by a broad flat nose; coarse jet-black hair, scarcely any eyebrows, and enormous ears, presenting a hideous physical aspect.

The Turkish Race has largely figured in history; and its deeds partake of the wild steppes from which its hordes made their desperate springs on Europe. Its tribes are scattered from the mouth of the Lena on the shores of the Arctic Ocean to the frontiers of Hungary and Northern and Eastern Africa, reaching into Europe on one side and Southern Asia on the other.

These tribes once received indiscriminately the name of Tartars; but, as the Turks are the leading people, it is proper to designate all related tribes by their name. They appear to be incapable of improvement. Living neighbors, or subjects, or conquerors of refined nations, they always have remained barbarians. They are equally unchanging in dialect; and the hordes which have been separated beyond the reach of tradition can converse with each other. The Turk of Constantinople finds no difficulty in being understood by a Yakut from Siberia or a Tartar from Astrachan.

The Turks first appeared to the northward of the Chinese provinces Shensi and Shansi probably about the beginning of our era, where, during a century, they engaged in a fierce war with the Chinese. Broken by famine, a portion united with the latter, and overthrew and expelled the other portion, who migrated westward. Tribes of Tungusian and Mongolian origin filled the vacuum thus created, to be in like manner expelled and thrown to the west in the third century, when the sullen sound of these hoarse human waves was first heard by Europeans. Turkish tribes inhabit the Russian provinces of Kazan, Astrachan, Siberia, and the Crimea. These are the Tartar hordes of the Czar. The language of the Crim-Tartar differs little from the Turk.

The *Turkomans* wander with their herds over

Northern Persia, Western Armenia, Southern Georgia, and the region east of the Caspian. They are a lively, intelligent people, who boast that they rest neither under the shadow of a tree nor the authority of a king. Their features are extremely Turanian; of a coppery hue, and their physique is more wiry and lithe than the Osmanli. From them the celebrated Seljukian Turks descended.

The USBEKS are a closely related people, though more agricultural. Their capital is Bukara, and their country very extensive.

The Turks of Turkestan are the remains of a once powerful nation, from which originated the celebrated Osmanli or Ottoman Turks, who are now the ruling class in all the Turkish possessions, numbering eleven or twelve millions, and forming the gentry and nobility of Turkey. Theirs is the polite and official language of Syria, Egypt, Tunis, and Tripoli, and is spoken through the southern provinces of Asiatic Russia, the provinces bordering the Caspian, and all Turkestan. In 1453 they conquered the eastern capital of the Roman Empire, and have since made the city of Constantine the capital of their European possessions.

The KIRGIS occupied the south of Siberia, between the rivers Tom and the Yenisei; but, in the beginning of the eighteenth century they were forced out by the Mongols, and now their hordes roam over the immense deserts or steppes of Great Tartary.

The YAKUTS are the most remote tribe of the Turkish family, and at the same time have preserved their language in purity. They are scattered on the borders of the Northern Ocean, over a country the most desolate in the world, where the mean temperature is 6° Reamur below freezing, and mercury is a solid two months in the year, and at the depth of a few feet, the earth is perpetually frozen.

There are many tribes of Turks or Tartars in Siberia; and the Kazan Turks in European Russia are interesting, as they are now changing from nomadic to agricultural life.

The Tungusians wander over the vast area from Lake Baikal to the Sea of Okotsk. Their original home is Daouria, north of Corea and China. They extend along the Amoor and Usuri Rivers to the shores of the Eastern Ocean. Under the government of Russia, according to the animal they have domesticated and use, they are called Dog, Horse, and Reindeer Tungusians. These roam over the trackless and interminable steppes, from the Yenisei to the Pacific Ocean. They are called Mandshus in China, having in 1644 conquered that immense empire, and ever since retained its government, filling all its offices, and being its soldiers.

The Tungusic language is the lowest of the Turanian family, being more unadvanced than the Chinese. In Mandshu there are numbers of words without distinctive terminations, being used for noun, verb, adverb, and particle. This is the only Tungusian dialect having a literature. They are more muscular, of heavier make, than the Chinese, and have a physiognomy expressive of larger views, and more determinateness of purpose. Their complexion varies; but the blonde, with blue eyes, light hair, and aquiline nose, is not rare.

The religion of the Mandshu is Buddhism; of the Osmanli and those they govern, Mohammedanism; and Christianity is professed in Siberia.

On the northern limits of Asia, and like scattered fragments between the hordes of other races and isles of the Pacific, tribes are found which formerly were not assigned to any class because so little known. These are the Ostiaks of the Yenisei, the Yakagers, Kamtschadales, Ainos, Coreans, the Japanese and Lew-Chew Islanders. From a careful comparison of dialects, remains found in mounds, customs, and fragmentary speech still existing, it has been concluded that over the vast region of Northern Asia, from the Lew-Chew Islands, Japan, the Kuriles, Aleutians, and Kamtchatka, one race, the Ainos, held barbarous possession. The Japanese and Lew-Chews have felt the influence of the Chinese from an early day.

The Ainos or Kurilians, who have given their name to this family, inhabit the eastern coast of Asia, and dependent islands. Ethnologically, this family resembles the other northern Asiatics, and their dialects are allied, especially the Aino, to the Samoiedes, and the nations of the Caucasus. The Japanese, who have, by the aid of Chinese civilization, and free infiltration of blood, advanced beyond all other members of this family, are described by travellers as a handsome people, with oval heads, regular features, and full round foreheads. Their language unquestionably places them in the Turanian class, and with the Tungusians.

It is through these northern Asiatics we pass to the Esquimaux of the New World, and from thence to all its other innumerable Indian tribes. The Tschuktschi and Koriaks resemble the Esquimaux in manners and language, and it is from this northern region, at Behring's Straits, or Aleutian Islands, that a connection exists facile for the passage of savages. From the Arctic Ocean across the equator to Terra-del-Fuego, the countless tribes into which the Indians are broken present a constant approach to one common type. In moral character and intellectual status, as well as in physical contour, they are alike. Humboldt says: "The Indians of New Spain have a general resemblance to those who inhabit Canada, Florida, Peru, and Brazil. They have the same swarthy, and copper color, straight and smooth hair, small head, squat body, long eye, with the corners directed upwards towards the temples, prominent cheek-bones, thick lips, expressive of gentleness in the mouth, strongly contrasted with a gloomy and severe look." "We think that we perceive them all to be descended from the same stock, notwithstanding the prodigious diversity of languages which separate them from one another."

There is a closer adherence to a common type between the most aberrant American tribes, than the numbers of the Turkic or Tamulic classes. The dialects of the American tribes do not differ as much as some authors endeavor to prove; and between those which make the widest departure there are generally connecting or intermediate forms. Few of these dialects have been carefully studied; and all of them are so subject to change, that a few years serves to render obsolete the old words, and introduce a new vocabulary. None of these have ever had a literature, none have an alphabet, and to foreigners is assigned the task of writing their sounds by the use of foreign letters. How vague and unsatisfactory this method must be to all except those who, with a theory already conceived, assert positively the absolute distinction of race between petty tribes! The dialects of the New World have been but partially studied; but the facts brought to light point to a common source. Many dialects are related by their vocabularies, others by their grammatical structures.

The idiom of the Indian dialects is very intricate, and among the most laborious and artfully contrived that any language possesses. Yet dialects as remote as those of the Incas of Peru, the Aztecs of Mexico, and the Six Nations of New York, maintain striking analogies in their constructional forms. The entire dissimilarity between the structure of the Indian dialect and the European, renders it almost impossible for an Indian to perfectly acquire the latter.

There are two reasons why their structure should remain alike, while their vocabularies are lost. Structure is far more permanent than words, and the aggluterative method of formation in all these dialects is unfavorable to the preservation of the original or root-word.

Barton has discovered "traces of the Samoiede dialects, unequivocally preserved in an immense portion of America;" and Vater has shown, "that in respect to most of the words denoting universal ideas, and sensible objects of perpetual recurrence, words may be found nearly resembling each other in some of the idioms of America, and some of those spoken in Northern Asia." The Indian skull is remarkably like that of the Asiatic or Turkic. Blumenbach pointed out their likeness. Humboldt asserts: "We cannot refuse to admit that the human species does not contain races resembling one another more nearly than the Americans, Mongols, Mandshus, and Malays." In physical traits, in morals and intellect, and his nomadic habits, the Indian resembles the Asiatic. The color of his skin and hair, his prominent cheek-bones, oblique eyelids, scanty beard, are peculiar marks of similarity.

There is every reason to consider that the Incas and Aztecs were branches of the American race; under the favorable auspices of soil and climate, they began a civilization of a unique and astonishing character; and, had they remained undisturbed, would have risen to the glory of the empires of classic renown. They constructed temples of hewn porphyry, measured the year, and properly divided it by the phases of the moon, possessed an advanced system of picture-writing, had literature composed of poetry and history, and a complicated government. Their traditions stated that they came from the north-west, in which they agree with the traditions of other tribes who refer their ancient homes in that direction.

The *Koriaks* of Asia, as before stated, are allied to the Esquimaux. The latter stand, according to Blumenbach, exactly intermediate between Mongolic and American races. The American form of skull, although distinct, has more points of resemblance to, than of difference from, the Asiatic type. Physical characters alone are not sufficiently marked to refer them either to the American or Asiatic families. Their language is allied to the American.

If the American Indians entered the New World from the north-west, the tribes left on their path of dispersion would partake more of the original type than those who were further removed. Thus the Celts, pushed furthest from the centre of the Indo-European nationalities, have lost almost every trace of their origin, while those Aryan tribes scattered in the Caucasus are closely allied to the Europeans and the Hindoos.

A volume might be filled by a mere enumeration of the tribes scattered from the Arctic Ocean to Terra-del-Fuego; but it were idle to tire the memory with the unpronounceable names of people who have no history; who can never have; who act no part in the magnificent drama of civilization. Like the wild animal, the Indian perishes by the contact of superior races. No effort, however benevolent and long-exerted, can preserve him. He will not be converted by missionaries, he will not labor, he will not be civilized. Hence, all that is desirable is to show them of common origin, and refer that origin to Asia.

The New World has not a single indication of having been the original home of this or of any race. There are no indications, as in the Old World, of an earlier preoccupying people. On the contrary, there is every indication of recent occupancy. A people thinly spread over a great wilderness will not advance, and there was no crowding in America. There had not been time for this to occur. The Indians were savages, having no domestic animal but the dog, which was little more than a tamed wolf. Their dialects were in the polysynthetic stage; they used only the simplest hieroglyphics; and had not achieved, except in Peru and Mexico, any degree of civilization. They had not had time to work out any great result.

The Caucasus presents many fragments of Turanian people, thrown off while the waves of that family were passing into Europe. The multitudinous dialects of this "Mountain of Languages" has been a perplexing subject to philologists. Many of these languages, spoken only by small and insignificant tribes, are wholly distinct, presenting scarcely a trace of affinity with any other. Only by the keen intellects of such students as Müller have the faint foot-prints of their origin been traced.

The famed Georgians and Circassians are the leading tribes of this region.

The Georgians

inhabit the country lying between the River Alazan and the Black Sea, the Kur, and the Caucasian Mountains. Some travellers have thrown doubts on the remarkable beauty of the Georgians; but it is conceded by the most reliable authorities that they are "tall, slender, of noble bearing, with regular features, aquiline nose, finely formed mouth, dark complexion, dark eyes and hair," and that the females are more beautiful than the Circassians, although not so fair. They appear to be descendants of the old Iberians and Colchians, and present a type of features eminently Aryan, and hence, according to our ideas, eminently beautiful.

THE ABASSIANS

are a pastoral and predatory people, inhabiting the north-western portion of the Caucasus. Their language has become distinct; and only by closest research can its affinity to

THE CIRCASSIAN

be determined. These term themselves Adigi. Their country is elevated, cold, and covered by vast forests. The men are tall, slender about the loins, with small feet, and uncommon strength, and possess a very martial bearing. Although the women are not all "Circassian beauties," there are proportionately a greater number that would pass for such than amongst any other polished nation. Their forms are universally elegant, their complexion white, and their hair soft brown or black.

There are a multitude of tribes classed under the names of Middle and Eastern Circassians, all of whom speak dialects emphatically their own, and all agreeing in their high-toned spirit of independence and their pastoral and lawless habits. Klaproth has traced these dialects, with great labor, to a common source, and shown that they are all related to the dialects of Northern Asia, and especially to the Finnic.

The map gives Russia dominion over all these tribes, but they are virtually free. They seem at a very remote period to have embraced Christianity; but now their religion is a strange mixture of Christianity, Mohammedanism, and Paganism. That the dialects of this mountainous region should so widely diverge from what must have been their common parentage, is not anomalous. It is what we should expect, and what is always found in such regions. A sparse population inhabiting vast forests, like the American Indians, or deserts like those of Africa, or isolated in narrow valleys by impassable mountain barriers, are left to themselves; and their mother-tongue becomes in a short time, by the natural growth of speech, a dead or rather obsolete dialect. The wonder is why all traces of a tongue do not more rapidly disappear; how the roots of words and grammatical forms are so tenaciously preserved.

CHAPTER IX.

THE SOUTH TURANIAN RACES.

The "Hill Tribes," or Dravidians of Hindostan. — Pritchard's Failure. — The Bhills. — Pariahs. — Gonds. — Peoples of the Valleys of the Ganges and Brahmapootra. — Siamese. — Taï Tribes. — Bengalese. — Thugs. — The Polynesians, From whence Dispersed ? — Malays. — They are the Nomads of the Sea. — Vast Geographical Extent of this Race. — Turanian Fragments in Africa. — Extent of Dispersion not an Argument against Community of Descent.

The Southern Branch of the vast Turanian family embraces the under-stratum of the population of the immense plains of Southern Asia, and thence extends over the islands of the South Sea. As in Europe, these races are there stratified one above the other. Vestiges only remain of the first; and the second is a conquered and persecuted race, only preserved from the Aryan Hindoos by the impregnable recesses of their jungles, or the deadly miasma of the districts they inhabit. They speak a language of their own, which is strongly Turanian, as is their physical structure. In India these are called the "Hill tribes," or *Dravidian* peoples. They live in a miserable condition, are outlawed and despised by the Hindoos, and so undeveloped that many tribes find it difficult to protect themselves against the tigers.

The Dravidian language possesses the traits of agglutination, grammatical structure, and vocalization, observed in the Finnic, which may be compared to the softest Dravidian dialects, while the Magyar may be compared to those roughest in consonants.

The debris of this race are found in the "heart of the Mahanuddy as far as Cape Cormorin, being the Bhills, Tudas, Meras, Coles, Gonds, the Soudrahs, Pariahs, &c. The second inhabit the northern section towards the Himalayas; such are the Radjis or Doms. The third occupy the angle that separates the two peninsulas of India, and which is distinguished by the name of Assam, as well as that mountainous band constituting the frontier between Bengal and Thibet, as well as the islands of Ceylon, the Maldives, and the Laquedives."

In no place has Pritchard, in his laborious work, so signally failed as in his description of the people of India. He describes them as though they were of one race.

Our knowledge has greatly extended since the date of his work, and light has been thrown on the unique system of castes prevalent in that country. It would be foreign to my aim to enter into a detail of tribes whose uncouth names are without interest. I desire to present only the salient features of each, so that a complete view may be obtained of the races of men as they exist at present.

The BHILLS are of short stature, their hair curls, and their lips are thick, and complexion very dark. The Meras, living in the mountains, resemble them. They must have been among the earliest tribes that entered India.

The PARIAHS have been subject to the Tamuls.

The latter have been a leading tribe. They show a strong affinity to the Mongolian or Turanian type. Their jaws and mouth are very prominent, their cheek-bones high and large, their nose is short and club-shaped, nostrils round, eyes small and half shut, their lids oblique, ears large, lips thick, beard deficient, and color brown.

They appear to have been the last tribe of Turanian stock that entered India. Their language has reached a grammatical perfection in advance of the Tungusic or Chinese; and they possessed a considerable civilization before exposed to Aryan influences, and hence have successfully resisted the Sanskrit dialect.

The GHONDES or KHONDES inhabit the dense forests reeking with miasma. They are in the lowest state of barbarism. Their foreheads are low and broad, eyes small, sunken, and reddish, thick lips, skin black, and hair reddish-black, and sometimes woolly. They present a picture of extreme ferocity.

The inhabitants of the north-east countries of India, the valleys of the Brahmapootra and the Ganges, are allied to the Tamuls and Thibetans. They are much lower socially and intellectually than the Tamuls, are more fierce and dependent on the chase, and have fewer religious observances. They are called Bhotîyas; and, although among the first tribes which entered India, from their position they were the last to surrender their independence. Among them is observed many of the curious customs by which their alliance is shown with the tribes of Polynesia, such as exposing their dead for four days on scaffolds, before burning them. The Bhotîyas inhabit the high declivities of the Himalayas to a height exceeding ten thousand feet. The foot of those mountains are peopled by tribes remarkably fine and healthy, although their country is so pestilential that no other human being can live in it. From this region the Bhotîyas spread into Burmah, along the Irrawaddy and Brahmapootra. Over all this vast area innumerable wild tribes are spread. Their language is much less advanced than the Tamulic, belonging to an earlier age.

The SIAMESE, Ahom, Laos, Khamti, and Kassia people, have received the distinctive name of Taï tribes.

Their country possesses advantages for agriculture, mining, and commerce, unsurpassed by any in the world; yet these vagabond races allow it to run to waste. The Anamese are remarkable for the perfection of the Turanian type which they present. The language of the Taï tribes is monosyllabic, like the Chinese, and is marked by a similar manner of musical accent or intonation.

The disagreement of travellers in regard to the morals and intellect of the East-Indians results from the diversity of races which exists there; but the prevailing idea is that they are, as a whole, a mild and orderly people, easily governed. If it were not so, 50,000 Englishmen could not hold, as they now do, 135,000,000 Hindoos in subjection.

In Bengal, each English magistrate has jurisdiction over a million men, and in Madras there is but one English official to half a million, and four districts where there is only one to 300,000. Yet, perhaps, there is no country in the world where more crime exists, or where it takes as horrid a form. There is no country in the world where the puerile distinctions of rank and birth are carried to so ruinous an extent, where poverty is so helpless and hopeless. The Turanian people are as savage as their brethren of the steppes of Tartary, and far more insidious and crafty. The Thugs, professional murderers, are drawn from their ranks.

THE POLYNESIANS [Malaic]. The groups of islands over the great Southern Ocean present many interesting facts in the study of mankind. Over this immense waste of waters, a peculiar race of men are disseminated. There is scarcely an island in all this expanse, however small, or newly raised above the sea, but is inhabited; and, although conforming to a common type, each of these isolated tribes have traits peculiar to themselves, and their dialects vary in every possible degree. This might be predicated, on consideration of the immense tracts of ocean which intervene between these islands, and the slight intercourse existing between members of different groups. A people of few wants have few words, and the fewer there are, the more liable of being lost. It has been a received theory that all these multitudinous tribes were descendants from Malays; but it is now rendered certain that at least three waves of people have been thrown over this expanse, the first being the Australian or Oriental Negro, and the last two Papuas or Polynesians proper, and Malays. I have already spoken of the former. The Polynesians are scattered over the islands between New Zealand and Easter Isle, north to the Sandwich, and westward to the New Hebrides, and as a mixed people over the entire expanse of Polynesia. They are a daring race of sailors, who will trust themselves, for weeks and months, on the frailest raft, to the winds and the sea. It has been conjectured that this people and the Malays descended from a great nationality once occupying these islands. Judging by words held in common, this anterior nationality had made considerable advance in agriculture and arts, understanding the use of gold and iron, to fabricate cloth, and had domesticated the buffalo, hog, duck, and fowl. To this early people the colossal images scattered over many of the Pacific Islands are referred. These races are the only ones that have been persistently cannibals.

From whence was this aboriginal race dispersed? If we go to the Hill tribes of Hindostan, we shall find the object of our search. They dwell on the low lands, — where the malaria is death to any other race, — despised and outlawed. Their customs are widely different from the Hindoos. They have no castes, widows remarry, they shed blood in their sacrifices, indulge in intoxication, bury and not burn their dead. Their institutions are peculiar; their religion, fetichism; and they occasionally indulge in cannibalism. This race once occupied all Southern Asia, as its western division did all Europe. They are the Dravidian Turanians.

By comparison of dialects, the languages of these Dravidians and the Polynesians are found to be related to the Chinese and Thibetans, and all the languages spoken by the yellow race. The closer alliance of ancient Thibetan and Burmese than their modern forms, indicates that they are parallel developments from a parent tongue, from which the Chinese originated.

By this alliance of the languages in the south-east of Asia, it becomes certain that the yellow race once occupied its whole extent. Even the wild tribes in the defiles of the Mountains of Assam, wherever they were driven by conquering Burmese, Chinese, or Aryans, by their monosyllabic language indicate their alliance to the yellow race.

Tribes remarkably similar to these wild clans of Assam, inhabit Malacca and Sumatra; mark themselves in tattoo every time they slay an enemy, as is observed in the Islands of the South Sea; and, as among the natives of Borneo, a young man must not wed until he has slain a certain number of enemies. A tribe in Assam expose their dead on scaffolds, as do many Polynesians, and those of the Sunda Islands. It is by comparison of languages that philologists are enabled to pronounce the trans-gangetic peninsula the cradle of the Malayo-Polynesian race.

The dialects of the sporadic islands of Polynesia cluster around the Siamese and Burman; but, in the ratio of their removal from this point, they become changed by mingling with other languages and isolation from the parent stock, and their original character in many instances is lost. A constant stream of Thibeto-Chinese were passing across the trans-gangetic peninsula, and dispersing over the Southern Ocean. The Dravidian tribes, issuing from the same stock, but at a remoter age, commingled with this stream as it flowed seaward.

But this Polynesian race had another element of

change added to this by the infiltration of the blood of the still older Oriental Negro, an Australian race, whom they everywhere met, and either dispersed or absorbed.

The Malays appear to have been the last wave sent off from the trans-gangetic peninsula. They are the nomads of the sea; a commercial people from immemorial time, who have occupied all the desirable positions in the South Sea, and rapidly extend their influence to the south and east. Their language is diffused over a wider area than any other, extending from Madagascar to Easter Isle, from Formosa to New Zealand, or over 70° latitude and 200° longitude. They first settled on the continent in 1160, and in the succeeding century embraced Mohammedanism, and have ever been zealous in propagating that faith. When they were confined to Sumatra, the Javanese were lords of the Indian Ocean, carrying on an extensive commerce, reaching Madagascar on one side, and Amboyna on the other. Restlessly they have extended themselves over this vast expanse, confined on the Asiatic shores by China, and from America by the vastness of the intervening ocean. The North Turanians are the wandering robbers of the desert and steppe; the Malay, his southern brother, the robber, the corsair of the sea.

There are fragments of the Turanian family existing so far removed that criticism has been active against their classification as such. Far down in the heart of Africa, between Lakes Yeou and Tsád, are a people known as Kanuri, of whose language Mr. Norris writes: "Its nouns are fully declined by past fixed syllables; its roots are not subject to any modifications; it forms its plural by adding a syllable; it has an accusative case; it uses pronominal affixes; it has negative verbs; and its verbs have distinct personal endings, which are, however, unconnected with existing pronouns. There appear also some traces of the Tartar vocalic harmony." This people are distinct from the negro, and even more congenial to the table lands of Asia than the deserts of Africa, so far have they preserved their ancestral physiognomy. We must be ready to admit that no dispersion, however wide, throws any objection to community of descent.

CHAPTER X.

THE ARYAN RACES.

Who are Aryans? — Origin of, and Attainments in Civilization before the Separation of its Component Races. — A Sketch of the Method of Linguistic Research. — The *Vendidad*, and Zend-avesta. — Date of the Foundation of the Median Empire. — INDIC BRANCH. — Prakrit, Sanskrit, and Zend. — The Gypsies. — THE IRANIC, or PERSIAN, BRANCH. — Effect of the religious system of ZOROASTER. — The Language of the MAGI. — Pure Persian. — The Afghans. — Buchars. — Kurds. — Belooches. — Armenians. — Assetes. — Parsees. — Guebres. — NORTHERN BRANCH. — Pelasgi. — Thracians. — Kelts. — Sclavonians. — Lithuranians. — THE TEUTONIC RACES. — Their History, Customs, and Languages. — From whence came the Waves of People that devastated Rome? — Goths. — Franks. — Saxons. — Alemanii. — Vandals, Longobards. — Huns. — Relations of Languages. — CONCLUSIONS.

THE greatest ethnological discovery of modern times is that which by comparative philology defines the boundaries of the Indo-European, or Aryan, races, and refers them to a common stock inhabiting the high lands of Asia. The blonde Scandinavian, the phlegmatic German, the irascible Kelt, the Sclavonic Russian, the energetic Anglo-American, the dreamy Hindoo, the Greek, the Latin, and the Persian, have been proved to belong to a common parentage.

The term Indo-European is more objectionable than Aryan. The latter is Sanskrit, and originally meant, "one who tills," in opposition to *Turanian*, which referred to the nomadic horsemen; but it came to mean, "noble," "of good family," as distinctive to Soudra and Pariah, ignoble and despised. This family contains the Indic [Hindus], Persian, Celtic, Italic, Illyric, Hellenic, Sclavonic, and Teutonic peoples.

The study of their dialects conclusively shows, that, before their separation, and previous to the departure of the first Celtic and Hindoo emigrations, they had attained the civilization of agricultural nomads. They had learned the art of ploughing, making roads, houses, ships; of spinning, weaving, sewing; and could count, at least, as far as a hundred, using the decimal system. They had domesticated the horse, cow, sheep, and dog; were acquainted with the most useful metals; and armed themselves with iron hatchets, &c. They recognized relationships, the marriage contract; they fixed by law the relations of right and wrong; framed rude governments of chieftancies. How is this known? How do we know that in the night of ages previous to historic ken, that, through the gates of the Caucasus poured the living waves of Kelts, Teutonians, Sclaves, and Lithuranians, driving before them the indigenous population? That the Pelasgi, the Phrygians, Lydians, and other nations, all rolled towards the west? That the almost fabled Pelasgi, reaching Italy and Greece, broke into Grecian and Latin tribes? Because, in all the diverse tongues which are classed as Aryan, from the old Norse of Iceland to the confines of Hindostan, the primitive names given to the above-mentioned domestic animals, metals, and objects, are identical in their elements. That a single name should be found in them all, applied to the same object, would be improbable; but that a great majority of such names should agree, is impossible on any other theory than that of a common origin, especially in the system of numbers and their names. The word for sheep, in Sanskrit, is *avis;* in Latin, *ovis;* in Greek, *ois.* For yoke, in Sanskrit, *jugam;* Latin, *jugam;* Greek, *zagon.*

This agreement runs entirely through these entire languages, forming a basis as sure as historic record from which to calculate the exact attainments they had made at the period of their separation. They could count, because all these nations count in the same manner. They made houses and carts, and used salt, and counted time by the lunar divisions of the year, because the names of all these are the same in all Aryan dialects.

The similarity extends deeper than words ; it enters into the structure, and all these dialects have almost identically the same grammar, showing that they had attained their present structure before the separation occurred. And, remarkable as it may appear, few, if any, roots have been added since that period ; the changes in the languages being only new combinations of existing elements.

The most ancient and sacred writings of the Persians, the *Vendidad,* places the home of their fathers in eastern Turkistan, at the source of the Oxus and Oaxartes. The Hindoos have no tradition relating to this subject. The earliest Vedic hymns show them to have been on the sources of the Indus, contending with, and vanquishing, the primitive Turanian tribes. The *Zend-avesta* agrees with the *Vendidad,* and even now the prevailing dialect of those countries, fixed upon as the source of these emigrations, is Aryan.

It is puerile to attempt to give the dates of these migrations. We can only give the order of their succession. Bunsen supposes the Aryans entered India from 4000 to 3000 B.C. Ducker places the formation of the Vedas at from 1800 to 1500 B. C., and Rawlinson places the emigrations which founded the Median Empire at from 1160 to 640 B. C. These dates, however, are not reliable. All we actually know is that the Aryan family was the last to appear on the stage. The Semite and Turanian had created great empires while they were still savages. But with this lateness of maturity came a vigor and power which soon placed the Aryan at the head of all the families of mankind. In science, in philosophy, in arts, in law, in all that goes to make civilization in its highest sense, they stand far in advance. Applying knowledge to the forces of nature, they have made bulwarks and fortifications of them, and, thus defended, bid defiance to the savage Turanian, who has so often overthrown the civilizations of the past. Only the inaccessibility of his haunts can save the Turanian, or even the lower members of the Aryan, from the sway of the higher. Thus it is that the European-Aryan meets the effeminate Indo-Aryan, and the latter is subjugated to the genius of the former. The Aryan is a proud and energetic race. Already its members talk of making their dialects the universal tongue; and one, at least, has extended its empire around the world.

From this ancestral Aryan people two great streams diverging, flowed, one over the Hindoo-Kosh into Hindostan, the other through the Caucasus into Europe. The first is called the southern, the latter the northern branch.

The southern branch is divided into INDIC, and Iranic. We have shown that a considerable advance was made before separation. The two branches, Iranic and Indic, remained united for a much longer time, and after their separation a close intimacy existed for a long period. This is shown by the words they hold in common, which the northern branch does not possess.

The ancient dialect of the *Indic* was the Sanskrit and Prakrit; that of the Iranic, the Zend.

Sanskrit with the Brahmin is still a living tongue, preserved in its purity. In it their sacred books are written, and thus hidden from the vulgar. The chronology of the Hindoos is a fable prompted by egotism. All we know of their early history is by comparison of the Sanskrit with the Zend, by which it appears that the two ran nearly parallel until the reformation of Zoroaster. When the Indic branch pushed through the Hindoo-Kosh, we have already seen how the Turanians were affected. We must, however, place a vast interval of time between the emigration of the latter and former. The Dravidian, or Turanian, had made a great advance from savage life before crushed by the stronger Aryan.

The Sanskrit, or its parent dialect, was the spoken language of the Indic branch when it entered India; and long ere the Greeks knew of the Indus, it had acquired its refined polish and cultivation. The description of Herodotus and Dionysius of this people is perfectly appropriate to-day, so completely stagnant have they remained since the great effort they put forth in the subjugation of the *Turanians*, who occupied the soil before them. The present Hindostanee dialects are outgrowths of the Sanskrit, as is shown by nine-tenths of its roots being referable to that tongue.

The Gypsies belong to this family, as proved by Grellman by the numerous words of their vocabulary which agree with Hindostanee, and especially with the idiom of the Bazeegurs. "Palas observes that the language of the Gypsies very much resembles that of the Hindoos. Resorting for the purpose of trade to Astrachan, from the Indian province of Multan, they entered Europe in the fifteenth century, and are now widely dispersed over Asia and Europe, and a few bands have crossed the ocean, and infest America. Their physiognomy is Eastern, their complexion dark, and their form like the Hindoos.

There are many clans of Kelts and Saxons who profess to be Gypsies, but they are distinguished by their *show* of work. They are tinkers, are itinerant cobblers, or peddlers. The Gypsy has discovered how to live without, and he will not under any emergency make the slightest effort. He prefers starvation. He regards the plodding laborer as his lawful prey. His vagabond race are without a history, and they deserve none. No race, not even the Jew, has preserved with greater tenacity their peculiar type. From the snows of Norway, through the mountains of Spain, to the burning sands of Africa, they speak the same language, are of nearly the same complexion, and have the same marauding habits. Everywhere despised and scorned, a foreigner wherever he pitches his tent, an outlaw, a jocky, a thief. The civilization and Christianity of the people among whom he is cast are nothing to him. He is the identical Pagan he was four hundred years ago when he entered Europe. It is said there are exceptions; and in Russia they follow the trade of the smith, and work in silver and gold; but it is doubtful if such are not spurious. Nor have they ever shown the least tendency to mingle with other races, and hence, with their roving habits, the preservation of type.

They have a tawny complexion, black piercing eyes, black hair, high cheek-bones, projecting jaws, narrow mouth, and agile form. The young women are occasionally pretty, but the men and old women are ugly.

Their morals are depraved. They accept alike all religions, as interest dictates; but they have no word to express the idea of God or immortality, and hence cannot have those ideas. Nor have they a literature, except fragments of rude songs handed down verbally from generation to generation. They are honest with one another; and, however rough and degraded, the females are chaste, even when panderers for others. Their whole number is computed at 5,000,000.

THE IRANIC, OR PERSIAN, BRANCH. The ancient dialect of Persia, the Zend, is most clearly allied to the Sanskrit. It is preserved in the sacred book called the Zend-avesta; in inscriptions of Cyrus, Darius, and Xerxes, in the Pehlevi; in the epic poem of Firdusi and the spoken language of Persia in its corrupted form.

Persia, the seat of the Iranic family, has been the battle-ground of contending races. Over its plains and mountains are scattered fragmentary tribes of the three great divisions of mankind. The Turanians and Semites are wanderers and traders; the Iranians are the tillers of the earth and the people of cities.

Could the mystery which involves the history of Persia previous to the reign of Cyrus the Great be penetrated, light would be thrown on the now obscure problem of the cause of the separation and origin of the Aryans. Persia, before his time, has no written history; but, like all other nations, she has a brilliant heroic age, "where Iemshid is said to have built the palaces of Istakhar, and Rustan fought upon his hippogriff against the warriors of Afrasiab." These traditions lose themselves in the dreamy clouds of the past. In the absence of positive proof of the existence of an ancient Persian Empire previous to historic time, it must be supposed, in accordance with the testimony of ancient Greek historians, and, as the traditions of the East imply, that the vast regions afterwards united under that powerful monarchy were occupied by a people similar in language and manners to the ancient Hindoos.

The religious system of Zoroaster, and the magnificent works of art, remains of which still exist in Iran; refined literature and poetry, vestiges of which are preserved,—all date from the foundation of the Medo-Persian Empire and hierarchy of the famous Magi. The language of the Magi bore similar relations to the common speech of the Persians that Sanskrit, the speech of the Brahmans, does to Hindostanee. It could not have been a foreign tongue, as the Magi were indigenous. It appears to have been the language of Media and Northen Persia. The Zend is closely related to Sanskrit, and they who used it as a vernacular idiom must have been closely allied to the Hindoos. The other dialects of Persia, although farther removed from the parent-stock, are unquestionably referable to the same source. One branch, the Parsee, bears a striking resemblance to the German, and may be considered as the connecting-link uniting the Gothic or German with the Primitive, or Pre-Sanskrit, tongue. The preservation of Zend and Sanskrit by a favored priestly class is exactly paralleled by the preservation of Latin by the Catholic Church. Had the latter had its own way, the Bible, its liturgies and hymns, would never have been translated, but have remained in the language in which they were composed. The sacred books of the Zend-avesta and Vedas represent the Zend and Sanskrit as they then existed; but, while they remained stationary, the vulgar tongue changed, until they became sealed books except to those who made them a daily study. So the Bible was written in the common tongue; but a few hundred years placed it beyond the knowledge of the vulgar.

Thus we see there is no necessity for supposing the Magi were of a foreign race. They rather grew out of the desire for a religious order to translate and expound the sacred books, a want which has been felt and met in all ages, and made themselves necessary by sealing those books from the vulgar.

The pure Persian presents a high Aryan type. His face is oval, features regular, complexion is usually brown, eyebrows long and black, eyes large and black, stature not tall. Allied to the Persian are many families whose importance necessitates their mention.

The Afghans are a numerous and powerful people, inhabiting the mountains to the north of the plains of the Indus, and the southern declivities of the Hindoo-Kosh. They are a rude and warlike race, with a striking Semitic cast of features. They call themselves Pushtun. Their language, the Pushtu, is spoken from the valley of Pishin to Kaffaristan. Although an unmixed race, they present great variations, according to the climate of their respective territories, from those on the low-lands of the Indus, who are almost black, to those of the high table-lands of the West who are as fair as Europeans.

Of their innumerable wandering hordes, the Duranis of Western Afghanistan are the most civilized. They are educated in Persian literature, and are strongly attached to their country, and their religion, which is the worship of the sun. Their holy city is Kandahar. Seven centuries ago, the Afghans overrun India, and inflicted the greatest cruelty on that unhappy land, until Tamerlane led the Mongolians, and swept the last Afghan dynasty away forever.

The Belooches inhabit the country lying between Afghanistan and the Indian Ocean, having Sind on the east, and Persia on the west. Over this vast territory roam the hordes of Belooches and Brahooés, the two great divisions into which this people are divided. The Belooches are pastoral, dwelling in felt-tents, and moving from place to place, as the necessities of pasturage or water indicate. The Brahooés, are still more wandering and savage, perpetually moving, though they prefer the high, cold mountain pastures. The language of the former is connected closely to the Persian, while that of the latter is more strongly allied to the Hindoo.

The Buchars are the dwellers in the towns of Great and Little Bucharia, between the Caspian Sea and the borders of China. They have been referred to Tartar origin; but Klaproth has shown them to be decidedly Persian. The cities of Balkh, Sarmarcand, and Bokhara have been, in the eyes of the people of the East, the wonder of the world. They have undoubtedly inhabited this region since the time of the ancient Persian Empire.

The Kurds inhabit the mountains of Kurdistan, and are scattered as far as the Persian Gulf, and into Russia. They are considered direct descendants from the Karduchians, mentioned by Xenophon. They are divided into nobles or rulers, and peasants. The latter are hard-featured, with sunken-eyes, and abrupt lines of face, and live in a state of great misery and oppression; but the former are a handsome people, with almost Grecian cast of features. Their language is a dialect of the Persian, with a mixture of Arabic and Turkish words. It is not taught in their schools, and has no written form.

They are warlike, and live by plunder, escaping to their mountain fastnesses. The Turkish government on the west, and the Persian on the east, are endeavoring with a strong hand to suppress their outrages, and, by a system of wholesale transplanting and denationalizing, will, in a short time, annihilate the race.

North of Persia, and stretching across the isthmus between the Black Sea and the Caspian, lie the Caucasus, or, as it has been termed by the Persians, "the mountain of languages." Through this isthmus flowed the great streams of Aryan and Turanian people into Europe; and all have left eddies or fragments in these mountain gorges. In Herodotus' time the same mixture prevailed, and Greek merchants passing that region were accompanied by seven interpreters speaking different languages. The Turanians are much the most numerous. Although nominally Russian territory, yet these mountaineers are virtually independent, and the Russian mails can only be carried by an armed escort.

Contiguous to this region lies Armenia, which from remotest ages has been the battle-field of contending races, often conquered by inferiors. Yet, in a remarkable manner, its people have preserved their rich intellectual and moral endowments, their religious systems, customs, manners, and language. Their origin is obscure. When they held intercourse with the Romans, they were already nearly the same as now. Strabo referred them to Greek origin; but his conclusions cannot be sustained. The facts he states are of more value. He says that the Armenians and Medes had the same worship and religious rites as the Persians, to which they added the licentious rites of Anaïtis. Their religion was that of the Magi, but is now a strange mixture of Christianity and paganism.

In the fifth century, Missrob invented an Armenian alphabet, and translated the Bible. From that date its literary history commences.

By conquest, voluntary and forced emigration, and their love of trade, the Armenians are widely scattered over Europe and Asia; yet they ever, like the Jew, look with longing eye and unchanged affection to their native land.

They are more honest and intelligent than their Turkish masters, and far superior in agriculture. They profess a corrupted Christian religion, for which they endure persecution and exile with great firmness. Their ancient tongue is a dead language, and differs so much from both the Iranic and Indic that some writers have considered it as distinct. It, however, is so closely allied to the Persian that Median words preserved by Herodotus can be explained by means of the Armenian.

The Armenians are a handsome, well-formed, sober, frugal, hospitable, and honest people.

THE OSSETES

Occupy the country north of Tiflis, and the valley of the Tiflis. They were, according to Georgian tradition, much more widely dispersed. Their customs and practices are strikingly like those of the German peasantry, so much so that they have been considered a fragment thrown off by the Teutonic wave as it passed the Caucasus. Their language inclines more to the Persian than the Teutonic. Klaproth considers them as descendants of the ancient Alani. According to Reineggs they are the Assæi of Pliny, who were ruled by women, and were celebrated for the manufacture of iron arms.

Our ideas of the true Persian must be drawn from the Parsees, who are the most direct descendants of the Fire-worshippers. When driven into exile, "they carried with them into India the religion, the hardy habits, and athletic forms of the north of Persia; and their posterity may still be recognized, with their mental and bodily powers unimpaired, after the residence of a thousand years in a burning climate." They are a brave and handsome people.

The Guebres are also descendants from the old Persian; but they have acquired, from their mixture with Mongolian or Chinese, an ugliness foreign to the old Persian type, as delineated in their sculptures, which present perfect European features. Their color varies with locality. The women of Persia and Afghanistan are, when not exposed, as white as Europeans; but the men are dark. It is stated that in the north provinces of Persia a slender form and blue eyes are characteristic of the females. In the south, especially on the low lands, a dark, almost black complexion prevails.

The northern branch of the Aryan family possesses more historic interest than all other races combined. To it belong the history, poetry, literature, arts, inventions, and the grandest civilizations of the ancient and modern world; the Greek, the Roman, and the various European empires.

The Pelasgi, almost a mythic people, appear to have belonged to the earliest Aryan waves, which, flowing south of the Black Sea, reached Italy and Greece. The accounts of Greek historians of this people are conflicting and inconsistent; even then they had sunk into the mists of time.

They were a peaceful race, and had the inherent love of architectural forms of beauty so conspicuous in the Greek. To them are referred the cyclopean structures, scattered over parts of Asia and Europe, massive but rude attempts to express ideas in stone. The most plausible theory of this race is that they were the first waves of Greek and Italian peoples, and were constantly succeeded by other emigrations of the same stock, pressed towards Europe, across the Hellespont and Bosphorus, by the Lydians and Phrygians; they entered Italy in two streams, one from Greece and the other over the Plains of the Po.

All these emigrations appear to have been of one stock, and the memory of the earlier have been lost in traditions so completely that they were considered by the Greeks to be the very children of the "black earth." In such a state of things, the historian and the student of races must needs yield to the confusion.

Pritchard has shown that the entire ancient population of Greece were Pelasgi, and that they spoke the Æolic dialect, which may be considered as the common original from which the other dialects were derived. It was a long time before the Greeks invented a name by which to distinguish their kindred tribes, to the exclusion of foreigners. When the term Hellenic was applied, it strictly designated tribes of unmixed blood; but the Romans used the name Græci for all those who spoke dialects of that language.

After the Peloponnesus had adopted this name, the Ionians still retained that of Pelasgi.

From these united emigrations sprung the Hellenic and Roman civilizations.

THE THRACIANS

Appear, by the intricate manner in which they blend with the Pelasgi, to have been of the same stock. The Greek and Latin languages indicate the relations of their respective races to the Iranic and Indic branches. The Sanskrit is a sister language from a common parentage. Before the separation occurred, or previous to the emigration of the Pelasgi, the connection of words teach what advancement had been made. They hold the name of a boat in common: but they had not invented sails, nor had they seen the sea; and they were more nomadic than agricultural.

Thinly spread over a large area of Europe and Asia, and the islands of the Mediterranean, they remained barbarous; concentrated in Greece and Italy, they began a splendid civilization. The Latin partakes deeply of an older stock than the Greek; but both run almost parallel courses with the Sanskrit. As races they avoid the mental stagnation of the Hindoos, and eagerly rush onward in quest of novelties, yielding poetry in its noblest form, and art in unrivalled beauty. The Lydians, Carians, and Thracians, by the manner in which they are all lost in the Pelasgi, appear to have been derived from a common parentage.

THE KELT.

A contempory wave of the great European immigration was that of the Kelts. Their language is considered to be, by many scholars, of an earlier date than Sanskrit, belonging directly to the ancient tongue from which Sanskrit also was derived. The hypothesis of Meyer, although entirely hypothetical, accounts for the facts connected with the migration of this people in a very clear and satisfactory manner. He supposes that they entered Europe in two streams: one passing through Syria, Egypt, and along the northern coast of the Mediterranean, entering Europe at the Straits of Gibraltar; the other passing on the north of Europe. Authentic history finds the Kelt from the northern regions of Scotland to the extreme south of Italy. In the third century, they capture Rome and enter Greece, Macedonia, and Thessaly, ravage Asia-Minor, and attack the Scythians.

The Kelts were a noisy and warring people, elastic but unenduring, with the restless folly of childhood, with vast hopes and fierce joys. With swift feet they overran Europe, and subjugated or destroyed the Turanian tribes which preoccupied that country.

They met the ocean, when it invaded them, with arms, and shot arrows at the lightning. Never to flee was a point of honor; and often they would not leave a house on fire, but perished in the flames. Of enormous appetites, their feasts rarely ended without a quarrel; for the thigh belonged to the bravest at the board, and to determine who was the bravest was the source of constant dispute. No people held life cheaper. They would, for a piece of money or a little wine, sell their lives. Next to fighting and feasting they loved tales of other lands, and would compel strangers to entertain them. They were great talkers themselves; and, in public assemblies, drawn swords only could secure the speaker a hearing. They were abandoned through levity, and at random ran blindly into the most licentious pleasures. They broke faith with a jest; had no idea of the obligations of a promise; and, until other blood was infused into their veins, so impatient of control and fickle were they, that they were incapable of founding permanent states.

The Kelts inhabited Europe from the earliest period spoken of in ancient history. Their mythology indicates their Eastern origin more unequivocally than their language. From Cæsar we learn that they were divided into three castes, corresponding to the priest, the warrior, and laborer among the Hindoos. The Brahmins of India are the exact counterpart of the *Druids*. Those wild priests of a wilder people are clothed with an impenetrable myth. They possessed the strongest hold on the imaginations of the people. They had no concern in warfare, nor were they subject, together with the rest of the people, to pay taxes. They enjoyed immunity from military and all other burdens. "By means of augury and the inspection of sacrifices, they foretell future events, and keep the multitude in awe." They were abettors in battle, the teachers of youth, and decided all légal questions which arose among a rude people. All knowledge flowed from them. They had sacred animals, and sometimes on their rude altars offered human sacrifices. Like the Hindoos, they burned their dead on funeral piles; and favorite animals, slaves, or relatives were consumed with the dead. From the earliest periods, they excelled in valor, and were eagerly engaged as mercenaries by the rulers of ancient times. They were extremely credulous, and thus the Druids fastened on them a terrible system of superstition. By the steady valor of the Romans and Teutons, they were subdued and absorbed. Their moral and intellectual traits have remained almost without change to the present; but nowhere, except in the Highlands of Scotland, is the Kelt described by Cæsar to be found. There they still have a ruddy complexion, light hair, and blue eyes, and are remarkably tall and athletic. There, too, they still wear the tartan garment. From their remains, it has been learned that they understood working in iron, gold, copper, bronze, ivory, and glass: that they used coins, constructed ships and houses and roads. They possessed an alphabet allied to the Greek; but none of their literature, if they ever had any, has been preserved. Philologists divide the Keltic tongues into *Kymric*, embracing the Welsh and Bas-Breton, and the *Gaelic*, embracing the Irish, the Gaelic of the Scotch-Highlander, and dialect of the Isle of Man.

THE SCLAVONIANS.

Over the vast country known to the Romans as Sarmatia, dwelt a people who have, in very recent times, excited the interest of the world by their rapid strides to civilization and power. These are the Sclavonians. They are divided into the Antes, comprising the Russians, and Sclavonian nations of Illyrium, and the *Sclavi,* comprising the Poles, Bohemians, Serbes, and Wends. The Sclavic languages show the structure of the Sanskrit, and are allied to the Latin and Greek. By this alliance, their origin is determined. In what degree they partook of the character of the old Sarmatian tribes cannot be determined, but it is probable that they aggregated out of them. They were unfortunately settled on the boundaries of Roman civilization, and their territories became the battle-ground between Rome and the barbarians. They were not warlike, but tillers of the soil; but on them fell the attacks of the hordes of Asia, on the east, and on the west, towards which they were crowded by the Huns, Turks, and Avars, they met the unflinching Teuton. But with a tenacity unparalleled, they have withstood all these invasions, and absorbed each wave of conquest, without being changed themselves. From 400, B. C., to 200, A. D., they slowly moved north and east, occupying the vast plains of Eastern Europe.

It is not until the sixth century we meet with the Sclaves in history. When the Longobards abandoned Hungary, the Avars took possession of that country, and assigned lands to their Sclavonic allies. The Sclaves in 552 occupied the country beyond the Danube, and their expeditions extend over Dalmatia, Illyria, Thrace, even to Constantinople. They partook of the immense movements of the Teutonic tribes; and, in the sixth and seventh centuries, they spread from the Danube to the German Ocean, occupying territories left by Teutonic tribes in their emigrations towards the west.

In the seventh century, the eastern Sclaves became attached to the south-eastern declivity of the Alps. The Russians belong to the eastern branch, and receive their name from a Scandinavian tribe who governed them for some centuries. From 582 to the eighth century, the western Sclaves overran Greece and contiguous states. In 623, they appeared on the Elbe. They settled Moravia, furnished the ancestors of the present Bohemians, founded cities and colonies on the North Sea, and from them sprang the Dalmatians, the Frankish Sclaves, the Saxon Sclaves, the Poles, the Slovaks, and Pomeranians.

Less bold and adventurous, and less moral than the Teutons, they evince, however, a tenacity of character which preserves, after all the conquests to which they have been subjected, and the mingling of nationalities, their peculiar type in its original purity. They have always fought well when forced to do so, but their inclinations have ever been towards peace. They were at first in advance of the Teutons in peaceful arts; and it is thought the word expressive of plough, as well as the use of that important instrument, was derived by the latter from their Sclavic neighbors. From the fifth to the ninth century, the Teutons held Western Germany, and the Sclaves eastern; and it was observed that the latter country was more powerful, and in every way more prosperous. They are remarkable for never having had great chieftains and leaders. There seemed more equality among the individuals than in any other race. Their progress was always slow, and now they appear to have only just entered on their career of civilization. The Russian Autocracy, having grasped the destinies of the Sclavic race, and, with the highest order of justice, removed the impediments of serfdom which has so long forbidden progress, will swiftly arise to its true place as one of the most powerful, enlightened, and commanding governments on the earth.

THE LITHURANIANS

Inhabit the eastern coast of the Baltic, from the Vistula to the Memel. They are a very early branch of the Sclavonic Family, and their language has not suffered so much change as other branches; so that it approaches the original Sanskrit in a wonderful degree. Early in the fourth century, they were brought to notice by their traffic in amber, and were recognized as distinct from the adjoining Sarmatians. They are divided into three branches: the Ancient Prussians, the Lithuranians, and the people of Kurland and Livonia. Of all the pagan nations, none resisted Christianity with so great pertinacity; and not until the thirteenth century were they subdued by the Teutonic Knights. They have been called the Windic family by Müller, and considered as a sister family of the Sclavonic. Very little of their literature has been transmitted, but their dialects are of great interest as presenting the earliest forms of Aryan speech.

THE TEUTONIC RACE.

We have come to the consideration of this last great family of mankind. We have left it until the last, because it is the great historic race of the present, and around it gather the ruling nationalities of the world. The history of this noble race begins, like that of all others, by the description of savage hordes scattered through the wilderness of Northern Europe. Germany as known to the Romans embraced the vast area comprised between the Rhine and Danube on the south, the ocean on the west, the Vistula on the east, and extended north indefinitely. The tribes scattered over this territory were divided by their dialects into three branches: the Lower and the Upper German, and Scandinavian. This division, so pertinent at present, was equally good two thousand years ago; and, so radical is the difference between these dialects, that the separation must have occurred before their departure from their original seat. The Upper, or classical German, is "harsh and deeply-toned, abounding in gutturals and imperfectly articulated consonants, and in deep diphthongal sounds, which stand in place of the softer dentals and palatines, and of the open vowels of the Lower German languages." Notwithstanding the softness of the Upper German in the classical speech, it remains the harshest dialect of Europe. This branch has been always distinguished by the name of Teutsch, or Deutsch, from whence is derived Teutonic. Long before the Christian era, the Teutons and Cimbri moved towards Gaul and Italy. In the second century, an indescribable confusion prevailed among the hordes of the Germanic forests. Constantly, fresh tribes were arriving from the East, pushed forward by an irresistible impulse on the boundaries of the Roman empire. Nations of warriors making inroads for the purpose of plunder; others advancing with their women, children, and herds; others transplanted by the Roman magistrates, as the safest and easiest method of their disposition. For seven centuries, commencing at least two hundred years before Christ, this immense flux and reflux of nationalities went on, producing the greatest mingling of races; and, beneath their irresistible human waves, the colossal Roman empire went down, and was trampled in the dust. It was not lost, however. The vigor of savage Teutonic blood, directed by Roman knowledge, exerts its strength in the civilization of the present.

Whence came these terrible surges of peoples? From the East. "We may suppose as probable that about 1200, B. C., some great internal popular movement, or some change in the physical conditions in Asia pressed the neighboring tribes upon the Teutonic races, and drove them to the country on the north of the Black Sea. From these provinces three great currents are believed to have flowed, in the fourth century, B. C., into Europe: one up the Dnieper to the countries on the Baltic, and still another up the Danube to the valley of the Rhine. From Scandinavia it is believed by some, that, in the third century, B. C., two streams flowed towards the south, one of which mingling with the Kelts, formed the nation of the Belgae, and the other forced out the whole nation of the Cimbri from Northern Europe upon the Roman empire."

There were four leading nationalities in ancient times: the Goths, Franks, Saxons, and Alemanns, besides the Vandals, Burgundians, Longobards, and innumerable other tribes. Of these the Goths were the first; but, weakened by the attacks of the Huns, and exposed to the enervation of Latin influence, they totally disappeared as a nation. The Vandals had a large infusion of Sclavonic blood; and, accepting the Semitic civilization of Africa, they perished under its influence. The Longobards preserved their purity for a much longer time, but mingled with the Kelts. The Burgundians, although remaining in purity still longer, mingled at length with Kelt and Sclave. The Franks preserved their purity still longer, and escaped the corruption of Rome. Of all these tribes, the Saxon, in his remote home in the north-west of Europe, was least contaminated with Latin corruption, and hence preserved the Teutonic blood in its greatest purity. In the eighth century, a great Teutonic empire under Charlemagne was founded. The ethnic condition of Europe at that time is most perplexing. Semitic, Teutonic, Sclavic, and Keltic tribes were scattered in wildest confusion, just as they were cast by the countless surges of peoples. From these have grown the present nationalities of Europe. But their evolution more properly belongs to the province of history.

The classical historians have left us fine descriptions of the Teutonic race. They were tall, powerful, with blonde complexions, light hair, and blue eyes. They were noted for personal dignity and boundless spirit of enterprise. They were trustful and confiding; reckless of their own lives, and cruel to their foes, with a burning desire for adventure, especially on the sea; greedy of booty, the table, and gaming. Of all the nations of antiquity, savage or civilized, they paid the most attention to women; and by them the spirit of mediæval chivalry was awakened, and the high position held at present by women acknowledged. To their love of the country, and detestation of the city, are referable the feudal castles where the lord held his court alone; for the Teuton was always arbitrary, and cherished slavery and difference of classes, but supported self government in the ruling order. The ancient Teuton was moral, but not religious. His religion was a scientific mythology, and he spent his ardor in the subtleties of law and government. But they were ready recipients of Christianity, and became a great power in its extension.

The German languages are intimately related to the Sanskrit; so much so that the attention of scholars was deeply awakened by the remarkable coincidences it presented, when attention was first directed to the subject. It is a sister, younger than the Kelt, of the Sanskrit and Prakit tongues.

CHAPTER XI.

NATURAL SELECTION IN THE ANIMAL WORLD.

The Exalted Position of Man. — The Arguments for the Origin of Species of Animals, by Natural Causes, apply to the Origin of Races of Men. — Consequences of the Introduction of one Being, and its Increase. — The Antagonist of Multiplication. — The Struggle for Life. — No Catastrophe, but Certain and Perpetual Change. — Illustrations. — The same Laws applicable to Past as to Present Beings. — The two Antagonistic Forces. — Selection by Man. — Wherein different from that of Nature. — Selection by Nature. — Application to Man.

MAN is the most highly developed being of the animal world. In preceding pages it has been shown that there is no difference in his organic structure or physical character from animals, and that even his mental endowments do not sever him from their realm. As a necessary deduction from these premises, any laws of development applicable to them must in like manner be applicable to him. As their laws of embryonic growth are his; as the organic changes in their systems are like those in his system, those of origin or derivation must be his: for the entire organic world is bound together into an indissoluble unity, which can only be explained by unity of descent.

I shall first introduce the facts connected with the origin of species of animals, and, from the principles they evolve, arise to the consideration of the origin of the races of men. It is presumable that life first appeared in a simple cell, or cellular mass, the lowest form of animal or vegetable life. Let us trace out the *probable* results which would inevitably flow from the introduction of such a cell-life on the globe, which at that time was, from internal heat, of a warm and equable climate from equator to the poles.

Let us suppose that this cell has the power of multiplication. It is well known that this takes place in the lower forms of life with far greater rapidity than among the higher. Ehrenberg estimates that a single individual of *Hydatina,* or Rotifer, or animalcule, is capable of multiplying to *seventeen millions* in twenty-four days. If we state the increase at only a hundred in a year,—allowing the earth to be 8,000 miles in diameter, its surface would contain 5,577,680,000,000,000 square feet,—at the end of the tenth year there would be 17,935 animals to every square foot of surface. If these multiplied a hundredfold the eleventh year, each square foot would contain 1,793,500, or nearly two millions of beings, and, the twentieth year, 1,793,500,000,000,000,000,000,000, or nearly two septillions.

Many fishes eject a million spawn in a single year. If all these were to mature, as they might under favorable circumstances, and in the absence of enemies, the second year they would number one million millions; the third year a million billions; the fourth year they would fill the ocean, and the vast majority of all offspring would inevitably perish in the fierce struggle for existence which would ensue. This immense reproductive power is held in common by the lower forms of living beings. Before other functions become differentiated, that of propagation seems to be the end of the being's existence.

The view of these appalling and incomprehensible numbers shows us at once that some antagonistic force, or forces, must be brought to bear against this increase of living forms. There are two powers at work: one creating, the other destroying.

We commence with a warm and equable climate, and a cellular being neither plant nor animal, a being like the *Protophyte, or Protozoa.* We have supposed it capable of multiplying a hundred-fold in a year; at the end of a score of years the earth becomes densely stocked. The almost universal sea is filled with this being. It teems at the equator and at the poles. What next occurs?

Malthus promulgated the doctrine that the increase of the human family was at a greater ratio than the production of food. Hence the supply of food set an impassable limit to the increase of man. This law applies with terrible force to the animal realm, which, having no foresight, are compelled to accept conditions as presented. Hence arises what Darwin so aptly terms the struggle for existence. This means, not a battle, but the silent combat between the weaker and the stronger, in which the weaker eventually perish.

The waters of the sea could not support all the beings which so rapidly sprang into life. The limit of its supporting power would be reached long ere the twentieth year of multiplication had been attained. Then the competition between the stronger and the weaker would commence. Although produced under similar circumstances, there would be a diversity among the individuals; and, when the vigorous had obtained their supply of food, there would be little or none left for the feeble. They would leave few or no offspring, and eventually perish. Only the strong survive and propagate. This statement appears very plain, and perfectly self-evident; but its adoption leads to what may be considered appalling results: for between this lowest form of life, and man, there is no break in the chain of beings. When we speak of transitions from one geological age to another as abrupt, or accompanied by great changes, it must not be supposed that these changes were violent or sudden. The sudden changes observed are the result of the imperfection of our knowledge of the geological record, not to the real rapidity of change. Lyell nobly proves that the laws of change in the inorganic world fully accounted for the changes revealed by geology, thus setting aside the wild theories of convulsion, of fiery and aqueous deluges, which filled the minds of men previous to his time. A similar work is required to destroy the notions of revolution and catastrophe in the realm of living beings, which, like a nightmare, broods over the minds of most scientists. There has been one PLAN, one code of action, pursued with unerring certainty; and the much-spoken-of catastrophes have had no more effect on the general tide of life, than the eruption of Ætna has on the civilization of the world. The terrific mountain piles, broken and distorted; the flexions and upheavings of the earth's crust; the upthrows and downthrows of faults,—at first suggest terrible and violent forces, acting at once and gigantically; but we learn that these are silent and inconceivably slow effects. The upheaving of a mountain may be the result of a hundred million years, and the bendings in the earth's crust may have begun myriads of ages ago, and, for aught we know, the mountains at this moment be rising, and the crust bending with as great rapidity as at any time in the past. Looking over the globe, we know that we see the entire catalogue of forces which have exerted themselves to change the crust of the earth actively at work, and performing exactly what we see performed in the past. Every day we have witnessed a day of catastrophe. Every day is a day of violent change.

If a mountain should rise one foot in a thousand years, it could not be detected, as our determination of the heights of mountains is too rough to appreciate so slight a change. But this rate would, geologically speaking, soon elevate the loftiest mountain range.

Equally is it true, that we see, every day, working after their own manner, the forces which produce change in the species of organic beings. Geologists talk of the gigantic coal flora springing into existence, as though before the coal there had been no plants; of the Saurian age, as though before there had been no Saurians, and that they died out entirely at the close of that period, and, in a similar manner, of all the periods they have seen fit to create. The truth is, that their ideal Saurian age, or age of gigantic mammals, completely run into each other, and are only broken because they can see but a fragment of each. The best idea entertained of the geological record is like that which would be obtained of numeration by an ignorant person, by writing the figures thus: 3, 4,———, 9,————20–21–22,———————65. What would that person know of numbers, and how vain would it be for him to theorize on catastrophes which had erased the intermediate numbers, or violently leaped the intervals by miracle or the action of unknown forces? A very little learning will make the subject plain, and show him that the breaks are not of nature, but of ignorance; that those numbers begin with one, and ascend by an inevitable law to the last figure.

If a savage should for the first time see the dial of a clock with the hands pointing to six, and, going away, return to find them pointing to twelve, as they apparently stood at rest when he left, and are at rest when he returns, he would at once refer their movement during his absence to a sudden and violent cause; whereas they were moving constantly with the same unerring and perpetual motion.

The laws which create and govern living beings are as immutable and eternal as those which govern inorganic matter; hence must have been the same a thousand million years ago as at present. These forces act in completeness around us, and their study reveals the method of specific variation in past forms.

Having thus shown that the being we have introduced on the globe stands at the foot of a graduating series of which man is at the head; that that series is without break; that violent and sudden change exists only in the mind; that the same laws hold to past as present forms, — we ask, Why is the admission that there is a *struggle for existence* fraught with so important consequences? Because by it organic changes can be accounted for.

The being which we supposed inhabiting the earth finds that the ocean cannot afford it sustenance. An unfavorable condition is introduced, — want of food. Will this destroy all, or only a part? It will destroy a part, and those the weaker. We never see two animals or plants alike; there is always diversity. But any change unfavorable to the being, when there is great competition, is fatal. On the other hand, any diversity favorable to the being confers the power to compete successfully. Hence all individuals gaining any thing are preserved, while those that lose are destroyed. If hereditary descent were impossible, the *race* of beings would gain nothing; for at death the acquisition would be lost, to be again acquired and lost by succeeding beings. But hereditary descent is possible. It is a potent force in fashioning organic forms.

There are two forces operating on every organism:

1. The conservative power of hereditary influences.

2. The force of surrounding conditions.

An organic being, as it stands animated with life, is the result of all the conditions and forces which have operated on all its ancestors. It is the concretion of these which it inherits and transmits to its offspring. So unerringly is this performed that it is proverbial; and we expect the offspring to be like the parent.

That the offspring varies within narrow limits, no one will dispute. The cause of such variations is not referable to chance; for, when every thing pursues the course prescribed by law, there can be no chance or accident. It is probable that these variations are results of the operation of conditions of life on the parent; in fact, they can be accounted for in no other manner.

Hereditary descent strives constantly to preserve the breed true to ancestral forms, while the conditions of life seek to modify and mould to new patterns. If the conditions of life were ever the same, then both the forces of descent and conditions would act harmoniously, and there would be no change; for hereditary descent is that which seeks to perpetuate the result of certain conditions, regardless of all others; and, were it not influenced in the embryo, circumstances might blot out, but they could not change specific forms. The embryonic being is influenced: if sufficiently to mature in harmony with the modifying influences, it is preserved; if not, it is remorselessly destroyed.

This method of destruction and preservation, turning on the slightest adaptations, is really the same as that pursued by man in his cultivation of the various varieties of plants and animals. In order to understand natural selection, we shall first study the method of man. Between it and that of Nature there are certain differences; but the principles involved are the same. The animals and plants called "domestic," are not found in nature, but are creations of man. They have been slowly evolved by the conditions imposed by man acting on their embryo to induce alterations, and then seizing on those changes which best suited his demands. When these domesticated animals or plants escape from cultivation, they rapidly degenerate, and often are unable to support themselves at all. Our horses, sheep and cattle do very well under the care of man in the latitude of the Great Lakes; but if by any accident man should be swept off, they would inevitably perish. They could not endure the first winter. So with our cultivated grains: they cannot hold their own against the weeds and grasses, except by the vigilance of man. It is for this reason that so soon as they escape to the feral state they lose the conditions by which man surrounds them, and by which they were formed; that they degenerate, or are destroyed.

It has been erroneously stated that when domestic breeds become feral, they revert to the original wild stock. Who can say what the wild stocks were? Have the horse and ox of South America reverted? Assuredly not to the quagga or aurock!

Perhaps no plant shows the effect of cultivation in inducing diversity more than the common cabbage. It was originally a rough-leaved plant, growing by the seaside; and still shows its original habits by the manurial effect of salt on its perfect maturing. Commonly, its leaves are compressed into an enormous solid head, which to the plant is of no benefit; and only through the care of the gardener in sheltering and transplanting the stump in the spring, are the seeds obtained. One variety, kale, does not form a head; but its large leaves grow vigorously apart. In another, brussels sprouts, the buds at the axis of the leaves are enlarged; from this last the transition is easy to cauliflower, which forms a head entirely of a consolidated and abortive mass of flower-buds. The Kohlrobi, at first sight, appears to be a consolidated head, but really is an enormously enlarged stem, at the expense of the leaves.

The turnip, if not a remote descendant of the cabbage, at least sports in numerous varieties.

The parsnip is derived from a wild and poisonous root.

All our fruits are derived from unpalatable wild stocks: the apple from the crab, the pear from the choky crab-pear, the cherry from the sloe, the peach from a poisonous shrub of Persia. Such have been the effects of cultivation; remove it, and the effects vanish, and only the original productions of Nature remain. She cannot furnish sustenance for these children of man.

Of our domestic animals much has been written, and their origin is one of the most unsettled problems of natural history. The sheep, dog, horse, ox, have been supposed by some authors to descend each from one original parent; while others suppose that each had many stocks: as instance one writer who thinks the sheep of England descended from at least nine original wild breeds or species.

There can be no doubt that the dog belongs to several species; but what great variations it has undergone! The bloodhound, bulldog, lapdog, greyhound, etc., do not exist in nature, but are strictly *creations* of man.

It is a received opinion that all the numerous varieties of pigeon are derived from the wild rock-pigeon; yet how great is the difference between a tumbler and pouter, a fan-tail and carrier!

No intelligent breeder will dispute the possibility of effecting great changes in animals. The shepherd, by selection, produces such a character as he desires, be it fine, coarse, long or short fleece, or proportion and weight of body. It is known that by skilful selection the Merino and Leicestershire breeds of sheep were produced. In regard to the pigeon, Sebright remarks that in three years he can produce a given feather; and in six, a prescribed form of head and bill.

The enormous prices paid for the prizes of Vermont flocks, and for those of celebrated foreign animals, prove how much proper selection has effected, governed by accurate scientific knowledge. The same principle has been at work, unconsciously, since savage man domesticated the first animal. He ever kept those individuals which best fulfilled his desires, and destroyed those which did not. This process is continued by the masses at present; each strives to obtain a good breed, without any forethought or knowledge of the method pursued in producing the best. Here and there a Collins or a Bakewell arises, who bring acute observation to bear on the subject, and in their own lifetimes produce very great changes.

The savage, allowing his animals to be at large in forest or plain, can exercise little influence in pairing.

All that he can do is to destroy the poorest. Hence their domestic animals, having to conform to climate and supply of food just as do wild animals, partake more of the character of species than those of civilized man. Change must go forward very slowly.

There has been no sudden change, but each one who reared an animal, or sowed a seed, has sought the best, and reserved the best; and hereditary descent has preserved every slight change, and handed it down to the offspring.

This selection differs from that of nature in being pursued directly and solely for the good of man, and having little or no relation to the welfare of the species on which it operated; while the latter aims only at the good of the species undergoing change. Very often what man calls improvements would be decidedly unfavorable to the animal if thrown from under his care. The Durham could not remain true to breed if turned into the wild; nor could any of our thoroughbreds. These changes have not been effected by the conditions of nature, and hence have no relations to the natural state of these animals. Man forestalls nature, and himself becomes the condition on which their existence depends. He selects from external indications, for he cannot from internal; and hence it is that while domestic races differ so widely in external form their anatomy remains unchanged. When the farmer observed the first parent of the celebrated "otter" sheep, he thought its short legs desirable, as it prevented its leaping fences. So he, by selection, produced a breed having short legs and long bodies. Such a form might be very desirable to the farmer, but to a flock of wild sheep it would insure destruction by wolves. Had such a lamb as the first of this breed been produced by a wild sheep, the first hungry fox or wolf would have killed it, and thus the breed have been at once destroyed. The farmer shelters the lamb; his pastures afford ready sustenance, and the short legs are not serious impediments to a lamb thus situated; but if wild, then, should it escape the fox and wolf, its short legs would seriously affect its scaling rocky heights and travelling over the scanty pastures, and, when brought in contact with longer legged rivals, would effectually insure its rapid extinction.

When fine wool became more desirable than short legs, this breed was suffered to die out, and not one is left. The King Charles spaniel has greatly changed since the age of that monarch, and the setter is believed to be derived from it. The races of dogs are highly differentiated and abnormal. The thoroughbred setter, in the wild state, would have a poor chance of catching game by setting for it. That habit has direct relation to the hunter following him. The poodle would fare still worse, and would probably become extinct by the second generation. The hound might maintain himself if thrown into the *wilds*.

If man, working for a short period, and, as it were, creating the necessary conditions, can effect so much; if he can with his imperfect knowledge and superficiality of observation blot out the parent types of all his domestic animals by the magnitude of the changes he effects, assuredly Nature, in the greatness of her power, her keen insight, taking advantage of the structure of a single muscular fibre, an atom of bone, or the color of a hair, during the elapse of millenniums of ages can compass changes incomparably greater. From the earliest dawn of life to the present, the vigilant eye of Nature has watched incessantly for the slightest variations. Those which yielded good to the being, have been and are preserved; and the new beings, thus having advantage over those which remain unchanged, supplant and extinguish them, to be in turn supplanted and extinguished.

"Natural selection will modify the structure of the young in relation to the parent, and of the parent in relation to the young. In social animals it will adapt the structure of each individual for the benefit of the community, if each in consequence profits by the selected change." — *Origin of the Species.*

To illustrate this process, suppose a family of wolves introduced into a country abounding with deer or other fleet game: Lamark would say the wolves, by constant pursuit, would develop muscularity, and thus become easily enabled to catch the game. This, in a measure, may be true; but the impress on their offspring by this constant chase would be incomparably greater. When there was scarcity, only the fleetest of these offspring would be preserved, the others being remorselessly cut off by hunger. Those who endured privation best, who were strongest and swiftest, would transmit those traits to their offspring.

We see this law of descent affecting remotest progeny; and great allowance must be made for its iron conservatism. It stores up every gain, and never loses an old form until a better is supplied.

I think the subject of natural selection will be understood, and its immense influence recognized, by this rude sketch. Darwin has developed the matter in an incomparable manner, and stands before the world as the Newton of Natural History. Here I can only sketch a few of his principles, which I desire to apply to man.

CHAPTER XII.

CONCLUSION.

The Geographical Seat of Man's Origin. — Natural Selection applied to Man.

THE original seat of man's origin "has been a vexed question," and as it has usually been discussed theologically, and not scientifically, little knowledge has been derived. Mankind, when first they became historically known, were distributed over the greater part of the Eastern hemisphere; yet they appear to have originated in a common centre, and traditions of different nations indicate that that centre of dispersion was located on the high central regions of Asia. From this area, all man's dogmatical knowledge, early inventions, and traditionary records emanate. Here the dog, the horse, ass, camel, ox, sheep, goat, cat, and gallinaceous fowls were first domesticated, and in and around it many of them still exist in a wild state. Here must have been the seat of man's first development, or these high lands must have afforded protection to a portion of mankind when a more ancient zoölogy was swept away by convulsions, of which mention is made by the traditions of all nations. The latter is probably the correct opinion; for we find this region skirted by lofty mountains, such as a people fleeing from destruction would naturally seek, and these still bear the sacred names which a grateful people would bestow. To the south of these highlands, far into the Indian Ocean, everywhere are written the records of the grandest and most prolonged convulsions, which probably gave rise to the myth of the Deluge. On the islands of the Indian Sea, which appear to be the crests of mountains rivalling Dhawalaghiri in height, and which may have escaped those convulsions which destroyed the then existing fauna, by depressing the land below the level of the sea, we find the PITHECUS, or *Orang-Outang*, in stature as large as a man, and in strength equalling eight or more, which from its strong human resemblance has received the name of "wild man of the wood," and which, of all brute creation, approximates nearest to man. Still more remarkable, on the eastern coast of this southern border, the transition from brute to man is made by degraded Papua tribes, cannibals so low in the scale of humanity, that in them gleams not a ray of spirituality or morality.

" Man probably originated near the Equator, where the climate was better adapted to his defenceless condition, and food abundant. If facts continue to support the present theory, that the Simiæ — man-like apes — of the Oceanic islands are a remnant of an earlier zoölogy, the seat of man's original development should be placed on the submerged continent, the tops of whose mountains those islands represent.

"If we admit that man derived his origin from the animal world, then that region whose fauna approaches *nearest the human* type should be the one to claim his birth. This fauna is the Asiatic, or

Asiatico-Oceanican. Thus the inductions of science beautifully harmonize with the sacred traditions of mankind."

Applying the principles which govern the production of species of animals to savage man, to whom the names brute or man are alike applicable, we shall endeavor to show how from this savage sprang the various races into which mankind are divided.

That any two savages should be born exactly alike, contradicts the experience of the present, no two individuals being precisely the same. Some of these individual characters will be preserved by offspring; others will perish with the individual. Which shall be preserved, which perish, is decided by the conditions which surround the individual. If he gain any thing by them over others who do not possess them, they, by giving greater vigor, and by imparting greater strength to his offspring, will be preserved; but, if he gain nothing by them, or, as is often the case, they are injurious to him, then they perish. Applying this general statement, we can see how much a savage, in his strife with beasts and other savages, would gain by superior strength, by swiftness of foot, by keenness of sight, and immeasurably more by predominant intellect. All these advantages would be constantly felt, but at some periods much more than others. When there is scarcity of game, the most wily hunter, he who has keenest sight, who is swiftest or strongest, secures and safely holds a supply of game, while less favored individuals perish. In these endowments we see an approach to animals, but in no case as great swiftness, as keen sight, or equal strength. This is because the pre-eminence of even savage man is based on mental and not physical superiority; and, according to the laws of correlation of mental and physical powers, as much as one gains the other must lose. All gain in intellect is so much loss to the body. From his type of organization, more especially his upright posture, strength sufficient to grapple with the denizens of the forest cannot be attained; and, from the same cause, equal swiftness is denied him. If, in the struggle for life, the existence of the savage wholly depended on these, the savage would certainly perish. He cannot equal, much less exceed them. But there are points in which he can equal them. In quickness of the senses, in endurance of vicissitudes of climate, of extremes of temperature, and the pangs of hunger, he is their equal. Savages are proverbial for quickness of sight and hearing; and, so acute is their sense of smell, that they are enabled to track animals by it with the certainty of the hound. The Esquimaux can withstand the temperature of freezing mercury. He can endure weeks of starvation, or gorge on a dozen pounds of blubber, washed down with a gallon of train oil. From the precarious means of subsistence afforded by hunting, the capabilities of enduring hunger is of material benefit. It is equally so to all carnivorous animals, and in all we find that the same endurance has been attained.

The acuteness of sense is connected with superior mentality, and points to greater dependence on mental acumen than physical powers. The savage cannot overtake his game by running, nor grapple with the less fleet, conquering by power of muscle; but he decoys them into pit-falls or ambuscades, and, by a mentality slightly surpassing them, he holds them all in his hand. The bent bow and reed arrow give him dominion. But of the vast duration necessary for him to acquire even these, I cannot speak. The club would be the first weapon for him to acquire, a weapon used by the man-like apes. Some chance may have discovered it; and we can readily comprehend how rapidly those who did not or could not use it must disappear before its possessors. This skill of invention introduces a new element into the struggle for existence, which, although pursuing the same course as that of Nature, in a measure sets it aside.

As man penetrated the wild in every direction from his primeval seat, he met diverse conditions. As the migration was extremely slow, no abrupt changes would be wrought; and the problem is more difficult to study than it would be were a tribe suddenly broken off and set in an entirely new climate. To simplify, let us suppose a clan of savages thus placed in a new locality. The negro is now in perfect equilibrium with the climate of the tropics; he has become so by insensible degrees. Let us suppose that previous to his acquirement of this adaptation, he is at once placed in torrid Africa, thus annulling the ages during which he has been acquiring his peculiarities. We will not consider him as a negro, but simply as a savage. The members of this clan are no more acclimated to the African climate than the European, but possess the hardy malleability of savages. When they are first introduced they are subject to fevers and other tropical diseases, of which many perish. The hardiest, or those favored by some peculiarity of constitution, survive and propagate. Offspring born under direct influence of opposing conditions are necessarily impressed by them. Those who do not conform eventually perish, while every gain in conformity is avariciously husbanded and multiplied in more vigorous offspring. The endurance of heat depends considerably on color; hence, as a dark skin is best able to endure heat, every increment of color would be preserved. The latest psychological researches show that form of body and cast of features are correlated with development of mind. The woolly hair of the negro is probably related to the color of skin. In a clan thus situated, every gain made by an individual in adaptation is a means of preservation, and those who do not or cannot conform inevitably perish.

The principle of "Natural Selection" applied to man is precisely the same as that whereby the hardy constitution of the Spanish Merino is acquired. These have long journeys to make from pasture to pasture, over desert mountain tracts, in performing which the weakest perish. Hence the strong are preserved; and this cause operating for ages has given this breed a surprising endurance.

Here we must remark that any gain, to be preserved, must confer a benefit, or be directly related to the wants of the individual. The albino peculiarity, which is of frequent occurrence among negroes, and all races, as well as animals, is seemingly the result of defective constitution, and, although said to have been in some cases hereditary, being detrimental to the well-being of the individual are never preserved. A school of naturalists seek to derive the white race from the black, through the albino, ignoring the defective constitution of the latter, whereby it rarely is capable of propagation. When exposed to the sun, the skin of the albino, born though he be under the tropics, blisters and cracks, instead of darkening, and his eyes cannot endure the light. A constitution worse adapted to his position cannot be imagined. Hence no albino race has ever been produced.

The same remarks apply to "porcupine men," and "six-fingered" individuals. These peculiarities are hereditarily transmitted for several generations, and might become permanent, no doubt, did the possession of a "porcupine skin," or of "six fingers," confer a vital superiority on their possessors.

Here we notice the difference between selection by man, and selection by Nature. Man selects according to his pleasure, and *supplies* the conditions necessary for preservation. Nature selects by *means of the conditions of preservation.* Hence, as there is no yielding of the means, her mandate is rigidly enforced, and every being out of harmony is lopped off.

This process of acclimation we can study in America. There was a frightful mortality with the first emigrants; even now, from one-half to three-fourths of the infants die before reaching the age of four years. Fa[illegible] customs may have something to do with this, but the great cause is climate. Already the American type is different from the European. The American is tall, spare, nervous, the opposite of his

Anglo-Saxon grandfather. Some high authorities, mistaking the operation of this principle, by which weaker forms are destroyed, predict that only by the constant emigration from the Old World can the white population of this continent be sustained.

Every gain in mentality, by conferring a greater superiority, would be preserved. The individuals who first united in tribes were greatly benefited thereby, and would supplant those who did not. So the acquisition of every new weapon, every new instrument, or of the canoe, would place the possessors above those who did not employ them. Hence, they could occupy the best localities, and become, in a measure, independent of the vicissitudes of the time.

It has been shown by history, founded on philological research, in previous pages, that the great races of mankind flowed out in broad streams from a common source. Our field is narrowed to the consideration of his origin from the highest members of the animal world. We have seen how his progress flows from the inevitable "struggle for existence."

1. The same plan is found to pervade the entire realm of organized beings; and man does not depart from the common type, but is its ideal attained.

2. There is no more difference between the lowest man and highest Simiæ than between the highest and lowest Simiæ, or between the lowest and highest man. There is a perfect gradation in bony structure and in brain.

3. History unites mankind at a common source;

locates their origin where the highest members of the animal kingdom are found.

4. "The struggle for existence" indicates the process by which the progress observed might have been evolved.

This "struggle" pervades all history; in fact, is its key. A people isolated, like the Australians, between a desert and an ocean, without competitors, remain stagnant. When scattered through vast forests, as the American Indians, the effort required to secure a mere subsistence is so great, that no energy remains for mental expansion. The fate of the Indian, who requires three thousand acres of forest for his support, is easily foreseen when he is brought in contact with the European, who by agriculture can maintain himself on a single acre. So speedily does he vanish, that it can scarcely be said that he offers any opposition to the invader. Crowded into narrow spaces, like the Grecian or Italian peninsulas, and subjected to excessive competition, superior civilizations flash out, the admiration of all coming time.

Darwin remarks that vast continental areas favor the multiplication of species of animals. The same holds good with man. See how the Negro of Africa, the Tartar of Asia, the Indian of America, break into innumerable tribes, differing widely in appearance and in language. But this belongs to the science of history, to which a future volume will be devoted, to which this is intended as an introduction.

BOOKS

ON

SPIRITUALISM,

PUBLISHED AND FOR SALE BY

WILLIAM WHITE & CO.,

AT THE

Banner of Light Office, No. 158 Washington Street,

BOSTON, MASS.

☞ Letter postage required on Books sent by Mail to the following Territories: Colorado, Idaho, Montana, Nevada, Utah.

WORKS ON SPIRITUALISM.

Arcana of Nature; or, the History and Laws of Creation. By Hudson Tuttle. 1st Vol. $1.25, postage 18 cents.

Arcana of Nature; or, the Philosophy of Spiritual Existence and of the Spirit-World. By Hudson Tuttle. 2d Vol. $1.25, postage 18 cents.

A Review of a Lecture by James Freeman Clarke, on the Religious Philosophy of Ralph Waldo Emerson, by Lizzie Doten, Inspirational Speaker, delivered in Lyceum Hall, Boston, on Sunday Evening, March 6th, 1865. 15 cents, postage free.

An Eye-Opener; or, Catholicism Unmasked. By a Catholic Priest. 50 cents, postage free.

A Letter to the Chestnut Street Congregational Church, Chelsea, Mass., in Reply to its Charges of having become a Reproach to the Cause of Truth, in consequence of a Change of Religious Belief. By John S. Adams. 15 cents, postage 2 cents.

A B C of Life. By A. B. Child, M. D. 25 cents, postage free.

Answers to Ever-Recurring Questions from the People. (A Sequel to the Penetralia.) By A. J. Davis. $1.50, postage 20 cents.

Blossoms of our Spring. A Poetic Work. By Hudson and Emma Tuttle. $1.00, postage 20 cents.

Davenport Brothers: their History, Travels, and Manifestations. Also, the Philosophy of Dark Circles, Ancient and Modern, by Orrin Abbot. 25 cents, postage free.

Free Thoughts concerning Religion; or, Nature versus Theology. By A. J. Davis. 15 cents, postage 2 cents.

Familiar Spirits, and Spiritual Manifestations; being a series of Articles by Dr. Enoch Pond, Professor in the Bangor Theological Seminary. With a Reply, by A. Bingham, Esq., of Boston. 15 cents, postage 4 cents.

Further Communications from the World of Spirits, on Subjects highly important to the Human Family. By Joshua, Solomon, and others. Paper 50 cents, postage 8 cents; cloth 75 cents, postage 12 cents.

Footfalls on the Boundary of Another World, with Narrative Illustrations. By Robert Dale Owen. $1.50, postage 20 cents.

Fugitive Wife. By Warren Chase. Paper 25 cents; cloth 50 cents, postage free.

Great Harmonia, in 5 Vols. By A. J. Davis. Vol. 1—The Physician. Vol. 2—The Teacher. Vol. 3—The Seer. Vol. 4—The Reformer. Vol. 5—The Thinker. $1.50 each, postage 20 cents each.

Gospel of Harmony. By Mrs. E. Goodrich Willard. 30 cents, postage 4 cents.

Harbinger of Health. By A. J. Davis. $1.50, postage 20 cents.

Harmonial Man; or, Thoughts for the Age. By A. J. Davis. Paper 50 cents, postage 6 cents; cloth 75 cents, postage 12 cents.

History and Philosophy of Evil. By A. J. Davis. Paper 40 cents, postage 6 cents; cloth 75 cents, postage 12 cents.

How and Why I became a Spiritualist. By Wash. A. Danskin. 75 cents, postage 12 cents.

Hymns of Progress; being a Compilation, original and selected, of Hymns, Songs and Readings, designed to meet a part of the Progressive Wants of the Age, in Church, Grove, Hall, Lyceum and School. By L. K. Coonley. 75 cents, postage 12 cents.

History of the Supernatural, in all Ages and Nations, and in all Churches, Christian and Pagan, demonstrating a Universal Faith. By Wm. Howitt. In 2 volumes. $3.00, postage 40 cents.

Intellectual Freedom; or, Emancipation from Mental and Physical Bondage. By Chas. S. Woodruff, M. D., author of "Legalized Prostitution," etc. 50 cents, postage free.

Incidents in my Life. By D. D. Home, with an Introduction by Judge Edmunds. $1.25, postage free.

Jesus of Nazareth; or, a True History of the Man called Jesus Christ, embracing his Parentage, his Youth, his Original Doctrines and Works, his Career as a Public Teacher and Physician of the People, &c. $2.00, postage free.

Kingdom of Heaven; or, the Golden Age. By E. W. Loveland. 75 cents, postage 12 cents.

Legalized Prostitution; or, Marriage as it Is, and Marriage as it Should Be, Philosophically considered. By Charles S. Woodruff, M. D. $1.00, postage 16 cents.

Life Line of the Lone One. By Warren Chase. $1.00, postage 16 cents.

Morning Lectures. Twenty Discourses delivered before the Friends of Progress in New York. By A. J. Davis. $1.75, postage free.

Magic Staff; an Autobiography of Andrew Jackson Davis. $1.75, postage 20 cents.

Messages from the Superior State. Communicated by John Murray, through J. M. Spear. 50 cents, postage 12 cents.

Man and his Relations. By Prof. S. B. Brittan. One elegant volume, 8vo., tinted laid paper, extra vellum cloth, bevelled boards, with steel engraved portrait. $3.50, postage free.

"Ministry of Angels" Realized. A Letter to the Edwards Congregational Church, Boston. By A. E. Newton. 20 cents, postage 2 cents.

New Testament Miracles and Modern Miracles. The comparative amount of evidence for each; the nature of both; testimony of a hundred witnesses. An Essay read before the Divinity School, Cambridge. By J. H. Fowler, 40 cents, postage 4 cents.

Penetralia; being Harmonial Answers to Important Questions. By A. J Davis. $1.75, postage 24 cents.

Philosophy of Special Providences. A Vision. By A. J. Davis. 15 cents, postage 2 cents.

Philosophy of Spiritual Intercourse; being an Explanation of Modern Mysteries. By A. J. Davis. Paper 60 cents, postage 6 cents; cloth $1.00, postage 12 cents.

Plain Guide to Spiritualism. A Spiritual Hand-Book. By Uriah Clark. Cloth $1.25, postage 16 cents.

Poems from the Inner Life. By Lizzie Doten. Full gilt $2.00, postage free; plain $1.25, postage 16 cents.

Poems. By Achsa W. Sprague. $1.50, postage 20 cents.

Psalms of Life: a Compilation of Psalms, Hymns, Chants, Anthems, &c., embodying the Spiritual and Progressive Sentiment of the present age. $1.25, postage 16 cents.

Philosophy of Creation: Unfolding the Laws of the Progressive Development of Nature, and embracing the Philosophy of Man Spirit, and the Spirit World. By Thomas Paine, through the hand of Horace Wood, medium. Paper 30 cents.

Religion of Manhood, or, The Age of Thought. By Dr. J. H. Robinson. Bound in muslin 75 cents, postage 12 cents.

Reply to the Rev. Dr. W. P. Lunt's Discourse against the Spiritual Philosophy. By Mrs. Elizabeth R. Torrey. 15 cents, postage 2 cents.

Ravalette. A Wonderful Story. By B. P. Randolph. $1.25, postage free.

Spiritual Sunday School Manual, for forming and conducting Sunday Schools on a new and simple plan, and for home use. Readings, Responses, Invocations, Questions, Lessons, Gems of Wisdom, Little Spiritual Stories, Infant Questions and Lessons, Songs and Hymns. By Uriah Clark. 144 pages, 30 cents, postage free.

Spirit Manifestations; being an Exposition of Views respecting the Principal Facts, Causes and Peculiarities involved, together with interesting Phenomenal Statements and Communications. By Adin Ballou. Paper 50 cents, postage 6 cents; cloth, 75 cents, postage 12 cents.

Soul Affinity. By A. B. Child, M. D. 20 cents, postage 2 cents.

Soul of Things; or, Psychometric Researches and Discoveries. By William and Elizabeth M. F. Denton. $1.50, postage 20 cents.

Spirit Minstrel. A Collection of Hymns and Music for the use of Spiritualists in their Circles and Public Meetings. Sixth Edition, enlarged. By J. B. Packard and J. S. Loveland. Board binding 50 cents, paper 35 cents, postage free.

Twelve Messages from the Spirit of John Quincy Adams through Joseph B. Stiles, medium, to Josiah Brigham. Gilt, $2.50; plain, $2.00, postage 32 cents.

The Bible: Is it of Divine Origin, Authority, and Influence? By S. J. Finney. Paper 25 cents, cloth 50 cents, postage 8 cents.

Voices of the Morning. Poems by Bell Bush. $1.25, postage free.

Wildfire Club. By Miss Emma Hardinge. $1.25, postage 20 cents.

Whatever Is, is Right. By A. B. Child, M. D. $1.00, postage 16 cents.

Whatever Is is Right, Vindicated; being a Letter to Cynthia Temple, briefly reviewing her Theory of "It isn't all right." By A. P. McCoombs. 10 cents, postage 2 cents.

Woodman's Three Lectures on Spiritualism, in Reply to William T. Dwight, D. D. 20 cents, postage 4 cents.

Woman and her Era. By Mrs. Eliza W. Farnham. 2 volumes, 12mo., nearly 800 pages. Plain muslin $3.00; extra gilt, $4.00, postage free.

MISCELLANEOUS AND REFORM WORKS.

A Sermon on False and True Theology. By Theodore Parker. 10 cents.

Art of Conversation, with Directions for Self-Education. $1.50, postage free.

American Crisis; or, The Trial and Triumph of Democracy. By Warren Chase. 20 cents, postage free.

Apocryphal New Testament. $1.00, postage 16 cents.

A Kiss for a Blow. By H. C. Wright. 50 cents.

A Will and a Way. From the German. Illustrated. $1.50.

Arabian Nights' Entertainments. $2.00.

Arbell's School Days. By Jane W. Hooper. Illustrated. $1.50.

A Strike for Freedom. By Mrs. Tuthill. 60 cents.

Broken Lights. An Inquiry into the Present Condition and Future Prospects of Religious Faith. By Frances Power Cobbe. $1.75, postage free.

Bears of Augustusburg. Illustrated. $1.50.

Belle and Lilly; or, The Golden Rule for Girls. Illustrated. $1.50.

Children's Friend. M. Berquin. Illustrated. $1.50.

Christ and the Pharisees upon the Sabbath. By a Student of Divinity. 20 cents, postage 4 cents.

Curability of Consumption demonstrated on Natural Principles. By Andrew Stone, M.D. $1.50, postage free.

Dick Rodney. Adventures of an Eton Boy. With Illustrations. $1.50.

Eight Historical and Critical Lectures on the Bible. By John Prince. $1.00, postage 16 cents.

Eliza Woodson; or, The Early Days of one of the World's Workers. A Story of American Life. $1.50, postage free.

Eugene Becklard's Physiological Mysteries and Revelations. 25 cents, postage 2 cents.

Effect of Slavery on the American People. By Theodore Parker. 10 cents.

Empire of the Mother over the Character and Destiny of the Race. By Henry C. Wright. Paper 35 cents, postage 4 cents; cloth 60 cents, postage 8 cents.

Errors of the Bible demonstrated by the Truths of Nature; or, Man's only Infallible Rule of Faith and Practice. By Henry C. Wright. Paper 30 cents, postage 4 cents; cloth 50 cents, postage 8 cents.

Florence Erwin's Three Homes. A Tale of North and South. $1.50.

Habits of Good Society. A Hand-Book of Etiquette for Ladies and Gentlemen. Large 12mo., elegant cloth binding. $1.75, postage free.

Hurrah for New England. Illustrated. 60 cents.

Ideal Attained. Being a Story of Two Steadfast Souls, and how they Won their Happiness and Lost it not. By Mrs. Eliza W. Farnham. 12mo. 510 pp. $2.00, postage free.

Kangaroo Hunters. By Anne Bowman. Illustrated. $1.50.

Koran. Translated into English immediately from the Original Arabic. $1.50, postage free.

Land of the Sun: Kate and Willie in Cuba. By Cornelia H. Jenks. Illustrated. 75 cents.

Love and Mock Love. By Geo. Stearns. Plain 30 cents; gilt 50 cents, postage 4 cents.

Life of Jesus. By Ernest Renan. Translated from the original French, by Charles Edwin Wilbour. $1.75, postage free.

Marriage and Parentage; or, The Reproductive Element in Man, as a Means to his Elevation and Happiness. By Henry C. Wright. $1.25, postage 20 cents.

Merry Tales for Little Folks. Illustrated. $1.50.

Mistake of Christendom; or, Jesus and his Gospel before Paul and Christianity. By George Stearns. $1.00, postage 16 cents.

Optimism, the Lesson of Ages. By Benjamin Blood. 75 cents, postage 12 cents.

Peterson's New Cook Book; or, Useful and Practical Receipts for the Housewife and the Uninitiated, containing Eight Hundred and Fifty-eight New and Original Receipts. $2.00, postage free.

Peculiar: A Tale of the Great Transition. By Epes Sargent. Price $1.75, postage free.

Personal Memoir of Daniel Drayton. Paper 25 cents; cloth 40 cents.

Peter the Whaler. By W. H. G. Kingston. Illustrated. $1.50.

Poems of Jean Ingelow. Elegantly bound, tinted paper, gilt top, &c. $1.50, postage free.

Poems of David Gray, with Memoir of his Life. Elegant cloth binding, tinted laid paper, with gilt top. $1.50, postage free.

Pathology of the Reproductive Organs. By Drs. Trall and Jackson. $4.00, postage 37 cents.

Playmate. 200 Engravings. $2.50.

Robin Hood and his Merry Foresters. By Stephen Parry. With Illustrations. 75 cents.

Report of an Extraordinary Church Trial: Conservatives versus Progressives. By Philo Hermes. 15 cents, postage 2 cents.

Revival of Religion which we need. By Theodore Parker. 10 cents.

Relation of Slavery to a Republican Form of Government. By Théodore Parker. 10 cents.

Salt Water; or, Sea Life. By W. H. G. Kingston. Illustrated. $1.50.

Swiss Family Robinson. $1.50.

Self-Abnegationist; or, Earth's True King and Queen. By Henry C. Wright. Paper 40 cents, postage 4 cents; cloth 65 cents, postage 8 cents.

Thirty-Two Wonders; or, The Skill displayed in the Miracles of Jesus. By Prof. M. Durais. Paper 30 cents, postage 2 cents; cloth 50 cents, postage 8 cents.

Twenty Discourses on Religion, Morals, Philosophy, and Metaphysics. By Cora L. V. Hatch. $1.00, postage 20 cents.

Unwelcome Child; or, The Crime of an Undesigned and Undesired Maternity. By Henry C. Wright. Paper 30 cents, postage 4 cents; cloth 50 cents, postage 8 cents.

Unconstitutionality of Slavery. By Lysander Spooner. Paper $1.00, postage 8 cents; cloth $1.50, postage 16 cents.

Wonderful Mirror. Engravings. 75 cents.

www.ingramcontent.com/pod-product-compliance
Lightning Source LLC
LaVergne TN
LVHW010248110826
845151LV00004B/1417
9781425523053